MAKING AN IMPACT

MAKING AN IMPACT

A Guide to EIA Law & Policy

By William Sheate

LONDON

Copyright © Sheate 1994

Published 1994 by Cameron May Ltd.

All rights reserved. Except for the quotation of short passages for the purpose of criticism and review, no part of this publication may be reproduced, stored in a retrieval system or transmitted, in any form or by any means, electronic, mechanical, photocopying, recording or otherwise, without prior permission of the publisher.

This book is sold subject to the condition that it shall not by way of trade or otherwise, be lent, re-sold, hired out, or otherwise circulated without the publishers prior consent in any form of binding or cover other than that which it is published and without a similar condition including this condition being imposed on the subsequent purchaser.

ISBN 1 874698 50 3

Printed by Watkiss Studios Ltd

William Sheate is an acknowledged EIA expert in the UK voluntary sector. Originally an ecologist, with an MSc in Environmental Technology, William has worked, lectured and published on environmental impact assessment for more than a decade. He is currently Assistant Secretary at the Council for the Protection of Rural England (CPRE), responsible for transport and EIA policy and campaigning, and is also a Visiting Lecturer in EIA at Imperial College Centre for Environmental Technology (University of London). He has a long-standing interest in the development of EIA legislation in the European Community. He is also co-author of CPRE's Campaigners' Guide to Road Proposals.

Acknowledgements

Special thanks are due to Ellen Teplitzky with whom the concept of this book was originally formulated, and Rob Cerny for his valuable comments on an early draft.

CONTENTS

Part I
EIA COMES OF AGE

Chapter 1 **Systematic Guesswork?** *10*

Chapter 2 **History Revisited** *13*
The rise of environmentalism
EIA in Europe

Part II
THE STORY SO FAR - PROJECT EIA

Chapter 3 **Principles** *22*
Basic principles
Questions of application
Which decision level?
Significance

Chapter 4 **Mechanisms: Transatlantic Contrasts** *34*
Introduction
EIA in the European Community
EIA in North America
United States of America
Canada

Chapter 5 **EIA in the United Kingdom** *48*
Introduction
Town and Country Planning Regulations
Infrastructure and other projects
Agriculture
General Development Order
Simplified Planning Zones and Enterprise Zones
Highways Regulations
Trunk roads and motorways
Local highway schemes
Electricity Regulations

Power stations
Overhead transmission lines
Afforestation Regulations
Land Drainage Regulations
Salmon Farming Regulations
Harbour Works Regulations

Chapter 6 **Public participation** *79*
Introduction
Public consultation in the UK
Public consultation and participation in the rest of the EC
Improving public participation
Case study: Broad Oak Reservoir
Freedom of Access to Information
Outside Europe:
United States
Developing countries
How it ought to be

Chapter 7 **Enforcement** *93*
Europe
North America
Mechanisms of enforcement

Chapter 8 **Post-project monitoring** *104*
Introduction
EC Directive
Espoo Convention on transboundary impacts
Australia

Chapter 9 **EIA and Conservation - Drawing the Threads Together** *109*
Introduction
'Pipeline' cases
Direct effect of the EIA Directive
Poor application of the Directive
Standing
Complaints to the European Commission

Part III
TREADING A NEW PATH - STRATEGIC ENVIRONMENTAL ASSESSMENT

Chapter 10 **The Tiered Approach** *130*
Introduction
Case study 1: Wilton Power Station, Teesside
Case study 2: Assessing the environmental impact of roads
Establishing SEA in Legislation
SEA in the EC
United Kingdom
United States of America
Strategic environmental assessment under NEPA
California
Canada
New Zealand

Chapter 11 **SEA in Practice** *153*
Introduction
Objectives
Options
Strategic environmental assessment
Procedure and methods
Transport
Motorway charging
Energy
Water
Policy appraisal and the environment
Development plans

Part IV
THE GLOBAL IMPERATIVE

Chapter 12 **The New Age of International Agreement** *178*
Introduction
Agenda 21
The European Community
Case study: The Burren
Espoo Conventionon Transboundary Impacts
UNECE Task Force, Developing countries

Chapter 13 **EIA and Pollution Control - The Convergence of Parallel Lines** *193*
Integrated Pollution Control (IPC)
Planning and Pollution
Integrated Pollution Prevention and Control (IPPC)
Case study: Implementing the Large Combustion Plants Directive

Chapter 14 **Back to the Future** *204*

References *208*

Appendix 1 **EC Directive 85/337/EEC - text** *216*

Appendix 2 **UNECE (Espoo) Convention on environmental impact assessment in a transboundary context** *228*

Table of cases *247*
Table of EU Legislation *249*
Table of Statutes *249*
Table of Statutory Instruments *251*

Index *253*

Addendum *257*

Part I
EIA COMES OF AGE

Chapter 1

SYSTEMATIC GUESSWORK?

This book is intended to tell a story - the story of Environmental Impact Assessment (EIA), where it has come from and where it is going. There is a real story to be told, but it has rarely been given the context it deserves.

The author makes no apologies for writing a book that presents a distinctly personal view of EIA law and policy. It is written from the point of view that EIA has far greater potential to deliver more environmentally sustainable decision-making than many are currently willing to acknowledge. Admittedly, EIA is no panacea and it has many limitations. But the paucity of imagination so common within government circles gives little cause for optimism that the concept of sustainable development (the environmental buzz-phrase of the 1990s) is really being taken seriously.

EIA, of course, is nothing new and, as the book points out, was an inevitable consequence of the politicisation of environmental concern. Just as project EIA was inevitable, so too is strategic environmental assessment (SEA), despite resistance from political short-termists.

Ten years ago the UK Government said it would never agree to the EC extending EIA to more strategic decision levels, those of policies, plans and programmes (Waldegrave, 1983):

> "....the Government would resist any suggestion that it incorporate an obligation on Member States to accept an extension of the scope of the Directive at some future date."

Today, much to the dismay of many in the environmental movement, that attitude has changed little, one Minister describing the early proposal for an EC SEA Directive as "half-baked" (Trippier, 1992). Accompanying the publication of the Deregulation Bill in January 1994 came the publication of the report of the Deregulation Task Force, including the astounding recommendation that existing EIA legislation should be "reconsidered" and any new EC proposals "vigorously resisted". Yet the Government also, apparently, sees the value of considering the environment in policy formulation [UK DoE, 1991a], and signed up at Rio to produce a National Sustainability Strategy. So why does effective EIA/SEA remain so elusive? This, among many issues, is the subject of discussion in this book.

The book is written in four parts. The first retraces some of the lessons of history as we come full circle in Europe in our discussions over SEA. The second part looks at where we are now with project EIA, how it works, how it could work, and its limitations. The third part looks at the rapidly developing field of strategic environmental assessment and how some of the limitations of project EIA can be resolved. The final part considers more recent developments, including the new international imperative and the much-needed closer development of EIA and pollution control.

The world of EIA is riddled with terminological inconsistencies. This book refers throughout to EIA (environmental impact assessment) although EA (environmental assessment) is used more widely in the European Community and the UK. However, EA in the United States is used to describe an early assessment of whether an EIA is required. The use of EIA therefore avoids confusion. Strategic environmental assessment (SEA) is now widely recognised as strategic forms of EIA.

The book has been written with a distinct European flavour and focus, but it also draws on EIA experience worldwide. It is intended to provide a reference text to EIA implementation in the UK, but hopefully also provides an understanding of the debate on EIA/SEA in the European Community (Union) and further afield.

No one book can hope to do justice to the enormous range of EIA application and experience, even when dealing with only the law and policy, and not the practice. It is hoped, however, that this selective and personal snapshot nonetheless provides an insight into those key aspects of EIA which will best help in the quest for a more environmentally sustainable approach to development in the future. EIA may not be a panacea, but without its widest application the worthy sentiments of the Earth Summit in Rio have little chance of ever being realised.

Chapter 2

HISTORY REVISITED

The rise of environmentalism

The 1960s and '70s saw a major development in environmental thinking. Environmentalism was nothing new; it had been around since the mid-nineteenth century in the guise of 'transcendentalists' such as Walt Whitman and Ralph Waldo Emerson in the United States and the 'anarchists' in Europe such as William Morris. The re-birth of environmentalism in the 1960s also took place among different factions, namely technocentrics and ecocentrics. The technocentric approach represented a belief in the ability of people to make the world a better place. The ecocentric drew on the ideologies of the previous century, essentially bioethics (the intrinsic value of nature) and self-reliance (the importance of community identity and participation in community affairs). Ecology began to take the political centre-stage in the late-sixties, no longer being seen as the preserve of the academic. A key group of ecological planners were espousing an essentially technocentrist environmental management approach, people such as McHarg:

> "Man is that uniquely conscious creature who can perceive and express. He must become the steward of the biosphere. To do this he must design with nature." (McHarg, 1969)

Other writers were addressing the rising concern with resource depletion and environmental pollution, writers such as Rachel Carson in 'Silent Spring' (1968), Paul Ehrlich (1972) and Garrett Hardin's controversial essay, the Tragedy of the Commons (1968). The Club of Rome's report 'The Limits to Growth' (Meadows et al, 1972) also set the environmental cat among the economic pigeons. The UN Conference on the Human

Environment, held in Stockholm in June 1972 provided a focus for many of these environmental concerns and led to the subsequent setting up of the UN Environment Programme (UNEP) to monitor environmental changes in the global commons.

It was within this context that Environmental Impact Assessment (EIA) was born. It was seen as a mechanism for reconciling economic growth with concern for the environment. Ecology and the environmental sciences were at last coming together with land-use planning to 'design with nature'. Ecologists had begun to produce some alarming statistics, for instance on species extinction, showing what was being done to the natural heritage. Links with economics were also being made, showing that poor environmental management could be costly in economic terms too, eg through soil erosion, chemical pesticides.

O'Riordan (1983) identifies four reasons why EIA gathered momentum. The first relates to the better scientific knowledge and publicity which alerted the general public to some of the dangers of developments and new technologies. The second reason was the increasing activity of pressure groups in the US and in the UK in particular. Their political effectiveness was enhanced by advances in scientific understanding and discovery, often undertaken by the pressure groups themselves, and the sympathetic media coverage being given to these new 'environmental' issues (eg anti-whaling, nuclear power). A third factor was undoubtedly the sheer scale of the resource-developments that were occurring, in a way which dwarfed previous activities. This was especially true in the energy, forestry and mineral fields resulting in environmental impacts never before envisaged. The fourth reason was that the previous three factors had made Western developed countries far more cautious and responsive to demand for better public debate. The pure technocentrist view was being challenged, it had been shown to be fallible (eg pesticides) and left wanting. It was being replaced by environmental managers who sought compromise between growth and environment. It is therefore not surprising that procedures were developed to address potential environmental impacts before they were allowed to happen. EIA was a natural consequence of the politicisation of the environment.

And so NEPA was born. In 1969 in the United States the National Environmental Policy Act was passed, an Act that was to set the EIA scene worldwide for the next two decades. For the first time, it introduced in legislation a requirement that an impact statement be made of the likely significant effects on the environment of major, federal actions. Australia introduced EIA in 1974 in its Environment Protection (Impact of Proposals) Act. In Europe, although a number of EC Member States had introduced their own EIA system during the late 1970s (West Germany, 1975; France, 1976), a formalised EC wide system was not introduced until 1985.

EIA in Europe

Many people reading this book, whether practitioners or on the receiving end of the EIA process, will not be familiar with the long and often tortuous history behind the development of EIA legislation in the European Community and the United Kingdom. However, as is so often the case, history can be enlightening about the present. Indeed, as far as the EC is concerned, history is already being revisited in the current debates about strategic environmental assessment (SEA). The idea of SEA is nothing new in the EC; the same debates were being had in the 1970s and now, twenty years on, are still being tossed into the arena. A detailed analysis of the history and development of the EIA Directive can be found elsewhere (Sheate, 1984), but some key events and issues in the past are worth examining since they shed considerable light on activities today.

It is instructive to look, briefly, at why the European Community ever got involved in environmental policy in the first place; the original Treaty of Rome was anything but an explicitly environmental treaty and in the 1970s, of course, reference was still to the European Economic Community (EEC). How quickly that has been forgotten now that, after the Maastricht Treaty, reference is supposed to be to the European Union (EU).

The objectives of the original treaty of Rome are set out in Article 2:

> "The Community shall have as its task, by establishing a common market and progressively approximating the economic policies of Member States, to promote throughout the Community a harmonious development of economic activities, a continuous and balanced expansion, an increase in stability, an accelerated raising of the standard of living and closer relations between the States belonging to it."

Part of the preamble to the Treaty of Rome also states:

> "Affirming as the essential objectives of their efforts the constant improvement of the living and working conditions of their peoples."

In theory, since there is no mention of the environment explicitly in the Treaty of Rome, environmental protection could only be implemented for the purposes of achieving the objectives of the Treaty, ie through the approximation of economic policies and the proper functioning of the common market. A suitably dynamic and, at times controversial (von Moltke, 1977) interpretation of the Treaty and its preamble enabled the Community to agree its First Programme of Action on the Environment in 1973 (OJ, 1973). In this, the provisions of the Treaty were qualified in the form of:

> "....in accordance with Article 2 of the Treaty .... which cannot now be imagined in the absence of an effective campaign to combat pollution and nuisances or of an improvement in the quality of life and the protection of the environment."

and

> "Whereas improvement in the quality of life and the protection of the natural environment are among the fundamental tasks of the Community; whereas it is therefore necessary to

implement a Community environment policy."

The First Action Programme was adopted by the Council of Ministers on 22 November 1973 in response to a call from the Heads of State and Government in 1972 to take action concerning the environment and that "economic expansion is not an end in itself." (CEC, 1972). At that meeting the Council accepted that:

"effects on the environment should be taken into account at the earliest possible stage in all technical planning and decision-making processes"

and

"that more account is taken of environmental aspects in town planning and land-use".

Over subsequent Action Programmes the emphasis on prevention rather than cure grew, and it was in that context that EIA came to be seen as central to the Community's environmental policy. Although many other aspects of the Community's environmental policy could be regarded as forms of fire-fighting (eg the setting of pollution emission limits which had to met within a certain time-scale) EIA was to be the cornerstone of a more preventive approach by the EC; after all, not only does it make good environmental sense, there are also good economic grounds for such an approach.

Early work on an EIA initiative in Europe began in 1975 with the Commission stating that an EIA procedure should be drawn up and adopted under the Second Action Programme (OJ, 1977). Coincidentally, a seminar was also organised at about the same time by the European Environmental Bureau and the European Council for Environmental Law (CEDE) in Louvain, Belgium to discuss ways of implementing environmental impact statements in Europe (Mitchell, 1975). The European Commission commissioned a number of reports on EIA, in particular from Manchester University (Lee and Wood, 1976, 1977, 1979) and later from the Batelle Institute (Batelle, 1978), on which a proposal for a Directive was eventually based.

Drafting of the Directive began internally in the Commission during 1977 and 1978, along with discussions in two meetings of a Group of Experts (Lee and Wood, 1984). In November 1979 (CEC, 1979) the Commission organised a symposium on EIA methods, the conclusions of which were to be used in drafting the proposed Directive. It was not until 1980, and after 20 internal drafts, that the proposal for the Directive was officially published (OJ, 1980).

The proposal for the Directive was intended to establish procedures for requiring EIA of certain public and private projects. This position had not been arrived at without considerable controversy, not least over whether project-level assessment was really the best place to start on an EIA initiative, or whether plans and programmes would not have been a more effective and appropriate level for Community-wide action.

The European Commission was at pains to secure a firm legal foothold for the EIA Directive since it was seen as the cornerstone of the Third Action Programme, and because it was intent on avoiding the weight of litigation experienced in the United States. It was felt that development at the project level had a more direct impact in terms of distortion of competition than did plans and programmes and therefore more readily justified under the Treaty of Rome (Stuffman, 1979). That assertion is in itself a moot point. When the draft Directive was first published in the Official Journal (OJ, 1980) the Commission appears to have been confident enough in the harmonisation basis for the Directive to have been able to dispense with Article 235 of the Treaty as a justification (which allows action to be taken where the Treaty has not made express provision) and depend solely on Article 100 (approximation of laws). However, when the Directive was finally agreed in 1985 Article 235 had reappeared in a supporting (or perhaps 'belt and braces') role.

There were, of course, other reasons why plans and programmes were not included. At the time there was little methodological expertise in assessing plans and programmes (though that was also to some extent true of projects) and the procedures for formulating plans and programmes were seen as being too disparate between Member States. However, this should not have been a real obstruction to progress. "The methodological objection to beginning with plan and programme assessment cannot be taken seriously..." (Wandesforde-Smith, 1978). Indeed, it was the development of the project EIA Directive which provided the impetus in many Member States and elsewhere to develop methodologies and practice for project EIA.

The final agreement of the project Directive in 1985 had been no easy matter, the UK and Denmark in particular having held out for some years with objections in principle or to parts of the Directive. The UK had continuously vetoed agreement until November 1983, by which time it had negotiated sufficient amendments to make it acceptable (or believed it had) and was under considerable pressure from other Member States and the House of Lords (who had produced a favourable and influential report on the proposed Directive)(UK House of Lords, 1981). The Danish eventually resolved their problems over the potential conflict with national Parliamentary decision-making over development projects.

The difficulties and controversies described above are just a taste of the many years of dispute over the draft Directive. Much debate centred around the detailed drafting of the text, especially the different nuances that could be read into different translations, but also the compatibility of terminology and detail between Member States; whether annex lists were appropriate; and the contents of the annex lists: which projects should be subject to mandatory assessment (Annex I) and which should be subject to assessment when likely to have significant environmental effects (Annex II). Agricultural projects were just one category which see-sawed between the annexes from one draft to another (Sheate and Macrory, 1989).

From the beginning, there was a general desire on behalf of the European Commission and Member States to avoid what was seen as the excessive litigation in the United States which had resulted from the EIA system established under their National Environmental Policy Act 1969 (NEPA). It was felt that the US focus on the scope and content of the environmental impact statement (EIS), and its prominence in the EIA process, was the cause of this litigation and therefore the Directive was drafted without explicit reference to a specific document, but instead refers simply to the provision of information which is to be taken into account in the decision-making process. Developers and Member States were keen to prevent the establishment of further sources of delay in obtaining project consent. In fact, it is quite probable that an EIA Directive would never have been agreed had this approach not been taken.

However, the European approach appears to have reflected a general misunderstanding of the US system of enforcing EIA legislation and the important procedural role of the EIS. Litigation has proved to be a crucial means of enforcing EIA requirements in the US and perhaps EC Member States should reflect on the fact that, 25 years later, they have yet to establish an equally effective means of enforcement.

Part II

THE STORY SO FAR - PROJECT EIA

Chapter 3

PRINCIPLES

Basic principles

A clear understanding of the principles underlying EIA is crucial to its effective implementation and application. Arguably, it has often been because of poor understanding of the principles of EIA, and of its limitations, that it has failed to achieve its real potential. There is no need, in discussion about principles, to distinguish between project EIA and strategic environmental assessment (SEA): the principles are common, or should be, to the application of EIA to all tiers of decision-making.

We can define Environmental Impact Assessment (EIA) in the following way:-

EIA is a process by which the likely significant effects of a proposal on the environment are identified, assessed and then taken into account by the consenting authority in the decision-making process. It provides the opportunity to take environmental considerations into account at the earliest opportunity before decisions are made about whether to proceed with a proposed development or action. EIA enables proposals to be modified in the light of potential impacts identified in order to eliminate or else mitigate them.

Four key principles should be recognised from the start. The first is that EIA is inherently procedural; EIA establishes a systematic procedure for incorporating environmental considerations into decision making. The second is that it is informational; the procedures created by EIA enable information about the environment to be provided to the decision making authority and the public in a clearly defined way. The third principle is that EIA is preventive; it should happen at the earliest opportunity in the decision-making process and before a consent decision is made. The fourth principle is that EIA is iterative; the information it provides feeds back into the EIA process and the design process of the activity concerned.

The recognition of these four principles should prevent misunderstanding over the potential of the EIA process to affect the outcomes of decision making. EIA is a procedure which ensures the provision of information about potential environmental impacts so that the decision making process is a more informed process. EIA is not, and should not, be the sole determinant of the decision to be made, but the decision should be one which is made more transparent by the EIA process.

Decision making remains an inherently political process; far from changing that, the transparency and public openness enabled by EIA makes decision-making, if anything, more political not less. Even if EIA indicated that a proposal would be highly damaging to the environment, a decision-maker could still decide to grant consent, given all the other factors that must be taken into account along with the environmental information. Since EIA is preventive, it is also central to the concept of sustainability. Although EIA does not determine the outcome, it does enable more environmentally-benign, or more environmentally sustainable, decisions to be taken and makes them more likely.

EIA theory and best practice indicates that the EIA process should involve:

*a description of the environment and the proposed activity

*the identification and assessment of likely significant impacts, both direct and indirect

23

*the avoidance of impacts wherever possible and the mitigation of impacts that cannot be avoided

*iteration - the EIA process should feed back into the design process so that impacts can be 'designed out' or minimised (or mitigated) through the design process

*the consideration of alternatives so that the best practicable environmental option (BPEO) can be identified

*adequate public participation and consultation before a consent decision is taken

The preamble to the EC Directive on EIA (85/337/EEC) spells out a number of these principles:

"....the best environmental policy consists in preventing the creation of pollution or nuisances at source, rather than subsequently trying to counteract their effects; whereas they [Member States] affirm the need to take effects on the environment into account at the earliest possible stage in all the technical planning and decision-making processes; whereas to that end, they provide for the implementation of procedures to evaluate such effects;"

"Whereas development consent for public and private projects which are likely to have significant effects on the environ ment should be granted only after prior assessment of the likely significant environmental effects of these projects has been carried out; whereas this assessment must be conducted on the basis of the appropriate information supplied by the developer, which may be supplemented by the authorities and by the people who may be concerned by the project in question;"

"Whereas the effects of a project on the environment must be assessed in order to take account of concerns to protect human health, to contribute by means of a better environment to the quality of life, to ensure maintenance of the diversity of species and to maintain the reproductive capacity of the ecosystem as a basic resource for life;"

Section 102 (2) of the US National Environmental Policy Act (NEPA) 1969 also states that:-

"All agencies of the Federal Government shall -

(A) Utilise a systematic, interdisciplinary approach which will insure the integrated use of the natural and social sciences and environmental design arts in planning and in decision-making which may have an impact on man's environment;

(B) identify and develop methods and procedures, in consultation with the Council on Environmental Quality established by title II of this Act, which will insure that presently unquantified environmental amenities and values may be given appropriate consideration in decision-making along with economic and technical considerations;

(C) include in every recommendation or report on proposals for legislation and other major Federal actions significantly affecting the quality of the human environment, a detailed statement by the responsible official on

(i) the environmental impact of the proposed action,

(ii) any adverse environmental effects which cannot be avoided should the proposal be implemented,

(iii) alternatives to the proposed action,

(iv) the relationship between local short-term uses of man's environment and the maintenance and enhancement of long-term productivity, and

(v) any irreversible and irretrievable commitments of resources which would be involved in the proposed action should it be implemented."

Experience suggests that EIA is not something that can be so easily bolted on to a consent process that it will be effective immediately. Since EIA is fundamentally about changing hearts and minds to a different way of doing things, it takes time and needs other changes, eg a suitable enforcement framework. Bolting on EIA to an existing consent process without other appropriate changes along the way often results in poor quality and ineffective EIA (see later Chapters). Too often, poor understanding of EIA principles results in poor mechanisms of implementation. That can mean that EIA risks being used as a justification for the project and as a public relations exercise, rather than as a realistic assessment of likely environmental impacts.

The need to change hearts and minds is one justification, among others, for requiring the developer to prepare the EIA documentation which is presented to the decision-making authority. There need be no fear of developer bias, providing a sound enforcement and quality control framework is also established. Without such a framework, however, this is a genuine and significant concern. It is crucial to the long-term success of EIA that developers themselves recognise the value of good EIAs and the importance of EIA iteration with the design process. This is much less likely to be achieved if the preparation of an EIS is given to a separate agency.

Questions of application

(i)   Which decision level?

It is clear from the discussion of basic principles above that EIA should occur at the earliest possible opportunity. The EC Directive makes this quite clear in the preamble. NEPA provides for EIA to be carried out as early as the making of legislation. We saw in Chapter 2 the lengthy debates over where to start in legislating for EIA in the European Community. Had it not been for the questionable legal basis on which the EC was embarking with environmental legislation, there is some likelihood that the EC would have attempted to establish a more comprehensive EIA system covering strategic level decision-making as well as project EIA. Although a number of Member States, including the UK, were sceptical about the value of EIA it is conceivable that the arguments for starting at plan and programme levels might have held sway, especially given the mythology in Europe that had built up over project level EIA in the US. Although NEPA made provision from the start for more strategic EIA it was inevitable that the focus in the first instance would be individual development proposals; they provide the most visible manifestation of environmental impact. However, the EC may have been able to make a virtue out of initially shunning project EIA in favour of plan and programme EIA, perhaps even policy EIA. The European Commission might also have done itself some favours had it introduced from the start widespread EIA requirements to its own activities, eg allocation of Structural Fund money to Member State regions for infrastructure projects and programmes.

So, one of the first questions of application is that of which decision levels EIA is to apply to. Experience in the EC suggests that project level EIA alone is insufficient. At the very least EIA should be applied to projects and programmes together to avoid the difficulties of having to distinguish between those categories (see Chapter 9), if the decision is taken to begin with a bottom-up approach rather than a top-down approach. Arguably though, EIA at policy and plan stage is a more effective level at which to introduced EIA for the first time since it has influence over decisions lower down the scale and is therefore more likely to make project-level decisions more environmentally sustainable in the long-term. Project level EIA is severely straight-jacketed by higher decision levels. If those decisions have not been determined through the EIA process they are less likely to be sustainable.

(ii)   Significance

The definition of EIA above refers to "significant effects". The question of what is meant by significance is central to an understanding of EIA and to its application in practice. EIA is not about all impacts or effects. It does not concern itself with trivial or minuscule effects. It is concerned only with those that are likely to be significant. Somehow significance has to be determined. The term 'significant' is the sort of term that courts are familiar with defining. However, in practice the question of significance cannot be determined in every case by reference to the courts. Guidelines are required to give an indication to decision-making authorities and to developers alike what is likely to be significant in a given situation. The question of significance has certainly given rise to considerable litigation in the US and has given rise to much thought and debate in the EC, though it has not yet specifically come before the UK courts (Alder, 1993).

When looking at existing EIA systems it is noticeable that many share the desire to establish certainty for proponents and authorities alike by creating lists of projects and/or by using thresholds and criteria for determining when EIA is required and for which projects. Conversely, a desire for the widest application of EIA is best reflected by requiring EIA for all projects likely to have a significant effect on the environment. This latter approach can be seen under NEPA in the US, in California and in Sweden.

The EC Directive, for example, establishes two lists of projects for which EIA may be required (see Appendix 1 for details). Thresholds are included for those major projects subject to mandatory EIA (Annex I), for example, thermal power stations over 300 MW. Member States, on the other hand, have some discretion in deciding when a project falling in Annex II is likely to have significant effects on the environment and therefore subject to EIA. Not surprisingly, many Member States have chosen to establish thresholds under which EIA is supposedly unnecessary. These thresholds can vary from being inflexible, as in the Netherlands, to indicative as in the UK and may be set at very high or very low values (further details can be found in Chapter 4). Furthermore, rigid thresholds may tempt developers and agencies to draft proposals just below the threshold.

This illustrates the problem created by attempts to list all activities which shall or may be subject to EIA. Inevitably some activities fall through the net. Far better, it would seem, to require EIA for all activities likely to have a significant effect on the environment and, if necessary, list only those activities which shall or may be exempt. This way, activities must be exempted by affirmative decision rather than possibly inadvertent omissions.

In order to maximise EIA application the only test should be the likelihood of significant effects on the environment. While this prevents loopholes it requires case by case interpretation. To facilitate this, screening criteria may be established which act as flexible guidelines for determining significance (for example: sensitivity of location, use of natural resources, presence of cultural heritage). Such criteria could, for example, be incorporated readily into the EC Directive as an alternative to the use of thresholds (CPRE, 1992), and indeed were in early drafts. The current (early 1994) internal draft of proposals by the Commission for amending the Directive (so far blocked by the Commissioners) has now taken this idea on board and includes such selection criteria.

In the UK, guidance on significance issued by the Department of the Environment (Circular 15/88) suggests that EIA would only be required for Annex II projects in three main types of case:

(i) for major projects of more than local importance;

(ii) "occasionally" for projects on a smaller scale which are proposed for particularly sensitive or vulnerable locations; and

(iii) "in a small number of cases" for projects with unusually complex and potentially adverse environmental effects.

This approach to significance is a rather narrow one and

29

regards 'significant' as meaning 'unusual' or 'exceptional'. A broader meaning of 'significant' might be 'of significance, something not merely trivial or insubstantial' (Alder, 1993).

Beyond these general criteria, the UK Government has chosen to use indicative, rather than rigid, thresholds and criteria. This has many advantages over fixed, rigid thresholds which prevent EIA being required for any project below the threshold or not meeting the criteria. At least it does in theory. In practice, both developers and local authorities can come to view the indicative thresholds as rigid. Developers may be more likely to appeal against a decision by a local authority to require an EIA for a project which falls below the indicative thresholds; local authorities may therefore be reluctant to require EIAs for such projects in the first place or, in some cases, local authorities may be unsure or unfamiliar with using the EIA regulations and guidance in practice (some local authorities have still had little experience of EIA). They may view the thresholds as being rigid not indicative.

In one particular example, the UK Government has recognised that thresholds are inappropriate for determining likely significant effects. This is in the case of the proposed requirement for EIA for trout (Salmonid) farms. New regulations under section 15 of the Planning and Compensation Act 1991, which introduced EIA into primary legislation for the first time (Sheate, 1992a), are to be published shortly. However, the Government consulted on the scope of these new regulations in 1992 and agreed in its consultation paper with the views of many environmental bodies, including the National Rivers Authority, that indicative thresholds would not be appropriate because of the widely diverse scale and nature of such trout farms which occur on the smallest and largest of streams and rivers. In fact, many of the problems are caused by comparatively small trout farms on relatively small streams. The fact that the Government chose to depend on the test of significance as the sole determinant of when EIA should be required is to be welcomed. It does, however, call into question why the Government is so determined to use thresholds for most other forms of development.

The UK Government has also favoured using statutory designations as criteria for helping to determine when a project is likely to have significant effects. Clearly, a project is more likely to have significant effects on the environment if it occurs inside a designated area, such as a Site of Special Scientific Interest (SSSI), an Area of Outstanding Natural Beauty (AONB) or a National Park than if it occured outside the area, since the designation describes the nature of the location. However, just because a project may occur outside a designated area does not mean that it would be unlikely to require EIA. In any case, there is a difficulty with projects occurring adjacent to a designated area, since they may have impacts on the designated area even if located outside. Designations inevitably downgrade those areas that are not designated, even though they may, in reality, be equally important. Without the non-designated environment, of course, the designated areas themselves become impoverished. But EIA is fundamentally about preventing or minimising significant environmental impacts wherever they occur. EIA contrasts strongly with the use of designation as a means of environmental protection. Designation is essentially an exclusive and prohibitive mechanism, whereas EIA is supposed to be inclusive and anticipative. It is unfortunate, therefore, that the widest application of EIA has often been frustrated by what is arguably the crudest form of environmental protection, that of designation.

Case study: Northern Swindon Development

An example of the difficulties inherent in determining significance can be seen in relation to the proposed Northern Swindon Development in Wiltshire. A proposal for 3,700 houses on 250 hectares (part of a larger 600 hectare development including industrial and commercial development, a new leisure centre, district and village centres, environmental improvements and new road links) was called in for determination by the Secretary of State for the Environment. On 20 May 1992 the Department of the Environment decided that the application by Crest Homes was not development in respect of the 1988 EIA Regulations, ie EIA was not required, even though the local planning authority had asked the Department of the Environment to require an EIA (UK DoE, 1992). The proposal was then passed back to the local planning authority (Thamesdown Borough Council) for determination.

It is hard to see how such a large development proposal could not be subject to EIA. The Government's guidance (Circular 15/88) gives little clear guidance on housing developments: the guidance is unclear about what constitutes 'urban development projects' (Schedule 2 (10)(b)), but 'industrial estate development projects' (Schedule 2 (10)(a)) may require EIA where the site area of the estate is in excess of 20 hectares. This development was intended to be the largest residential development in Europe yet escaped the requirements for EIA.

The question is whether the Secretary of State, under the EC Directive, has complete discretion, or whether any proposed project falling under a category covered by the Directive must be subject to EIA where it is likely to have a significant effect on the environment (Articles 2 and 4). The discretion conferred by article 4.2 should be read in conjunction with article 2 which requires that

> "before consent is given, projects likely to have significant effects on the environment .... are made subject to an assessment with regard to their effects."

If this interpretation is the correct one, and it has been argued in other cases by the Commission (Williams, 1991), the Directive could be said to have direct effect in this case (see Chapter 8 for more discussion on direct effect). Arguably, the discretion given to Member States is only over the mechanisms to be employed for identifying those projects which are likely to have significant effects, eg thresholds or broad criteria, so that any project falling within the categories of Annex II which was likely to have significant effects would be caught by the mechanisms established. Although the mechanisms might vary from one Member State to another projects likely to have significant effects would be caught whichever country they occured in. So, according to this line of reasoning, significance should be seen as an objective test which exists independently of the mechanism established for identifying it. Whatever the correct legal interpretation, it seems inconceivable that a project of this scale, nature and location (there are, for example, considerable water resource and sewerage infrastructure problems within the area) should not be subject to EIA.

Chapter 4

MECHANISMS: TRANSATLANTIC CONTRASTS

Introduction

There are a number of legislative mechanisms that are commonly utilised in the implementation of an EIA system. This chapter looks at some of the differences and similarities between different systems, most notably between the US approach and that of the EC. An understanding of how EIA generally can and should operate provides a useful starting point for considering the effectiveness of any particular EIA system. We begin with the European Community.

EIA in the European Community

The European Community (EC) Directive 85/337/EEC (see Appendix 1) on the assessment of the effects of certain public and private projects on the environment, was agreed and notified to Member States in July 1985 and formal compliance was due on 3 July 1988. Although legally confined to EC Member States a number of other European countries have chosen to establish similar procedures or are considering doing so. The Directive is a procedural one, which seeks to ensure that before a decision is made about whether consent should be given to go ahead with a development a minimum level of information about the likely significant effects on the environment has been provided to the 'competent authority' (for example, a local authority or Government Minister) making the decision. It does not in itself require a Member State to refuse to give consent for a project even if it is likely to be highly damaging to the environment. In principle, the Directive applies equally across all policy sectors by providing a framework within which Member States must act.

Projects likely to have significant effects on the environment by virtue *inter alia* of their nature, size or location must be made subject to an assessment of their effects before consent is given. There are two lists of projects: Annex I projects require EIA in all cases and include major chemical works, power stations, motorways etc.; Annex II projects must be subject to assessment where Member States consider their characteristics so require. Annex II covers the majority of development projects subject to various criteria and thresholds according to the individual Member State. This leads to considerable variation throughout the EC in the extent to which the Directive is implemented and its effectiveness in requiring EIA for any project likely to have significant effects on the environment -the ultimate test. Inevitably, these discrepancies in implementation occur both within sectors and among sectors across the Community. The direct and indirect effects of the proposed project on the following four factors must be identified, described and assessed, where appropriate:

- human beings, fauna and flora;

- soil, water, air, climate and the landscape;

- the interaction between the first two groups;

- material assets and the cultural heritage.

Information supplied by the developer and gathered as a result of consultations must be taken into account in the decision-making process. Although the Directive studiously avoids reference to a formal impact statement, such a document is mentioned in the implementing legislation of many Member States. The developer must supply a minimum level of information and may supply additional information where appropriate. The minimum information is:

- a description of the project with information on site, design and size;

- the data required to identify and assess the main effects

which the project is likely to have on the environment;

- a description of the measures envisaged to avoid, reduce and possibly remedy significant adverse effects;

- a non-technical summary of the above information.

Annex 3 provides further guidance on information to be supplied, including where appropriate an outline of the main alternatives studied and the reasons for the developer's choice. The description of effects should consider direct effects and any "indirect, secondary, cumulative, short, medium and long term, permanent and temporary, positive and negative effects of the project".

The public must be consulted before the project is initiated (Article 6(2)), though not necessarily earlier, ie before consent is given. However, there is some confusion here since Article 8 requires information gathered pursuant to Articles 5, 6 and 7 to be taken into consideration in the development consent procedure. That would imply that the public must be consulted before <u>consent</u> is given, not just before the project is <u>initiated</u>. Any request for development consent and the information supplied by the developer must also be made public. There are also arrangements for consulting other Member States where a project is likely to have transboundary impacts. The decision and reasons must also be made public.

The Directive requires the European Commission to publish a report on the application and effectiveness of the Directive after five years from notification. This five-year review report was due in July 1990, but was only published in April 1993 (Commission of the European Communities, 1993). The Commission is required to send the report to the European Parliament and the Council. The publication was delayed well beyond its intended date of 3 July 1990, partly through delays in implementation, but also as a result of delays within the Commission and the need to gather Member States' comments on the draft report. If the Commission is to produce future reviews - and it could sensibly amend the Directive to require regular five-year reviews - it will need to report more punctually if it is to be of real value. The onus is as much on Member States to approve the report as it is on the Commission to produce the report quickly.

The Commission decided that the review should focus on:

1. The extent of formal compliance by Member States with the requirements of the Directive.

2. The criteria and/or thresholds adopted by Member States for the selection of Annex II projects to be subject to assessment.

3. The nature and extent of practical compliance by Member States with the requirements of the Directive.

4. Key aspects of EIA practice (notably use of scoping, review of EIA studies, monitoring of implementation and post-auditing of EIA studies, provision of guidelines, and provision of training facilities).

5. Overall assessment of the effectiveness of the Directive's implementation, and difficulties in its implementation.

The review was compiled using consultants in each Member State carrying out consultations with government departments, practitioners and interest groups in each country. The result was a main report which addressed the objectives above and separate annexes giving detail of implementation for each Member State (ie Volume 1: Main report and annex for Belgium, and so on for 12 volumes; Volume 13 is a single volume containing the annexes for all Member States).

The review produced a useful snapshot of implementation throughout the Community as of 1991. The lengthy delays in publishing the final report, however, made the detail somewhat less useful than might otherwise have been the case had it been published on time.

Particularly interesting are the comparisons of Member States' use of criteria and thresholds and systems for quality control of documentation (environmental statements). It throws into sharp perspective, for instance, the shortcomings of the often much-praised Netherlands EIA system. While quality control of the process is better in the Netherlands than many other Member States, as a result of its EIA Commission, this is aided by the fact that the number of projects subjected to EIA is comparatively small. Thresholds for determining which Annex II projects should be subject to EIA are invariably set high, often much higher than some other Member States. The diversity of thresholds (rigid or indicative) used by Member States for selecting certain categories of project is revealing and raises questions as to whether the Directive as implemented is really achieving its wider harmonisation objectives. This problem is clearly illustrated by the thresholds applied to pig rearing installations, for example. In Greece EIA is required for a project which is to house only 20 pigs, in Ireland the threshold is 1000 pigs, Germany 1400 and the UK, 5000 pigs. Are Greek pigs so much more environmentally destructive than those in the UK? Similar disparities can be seen for quarries (France, 5 ha or more; UK, 50 ha; Netherlands, 100 ha) and installations for the disposal of industrial and domestic waste (Ireland and Netherlands, capacity of 25,000 tonnes or more per annum; UK, 75,000 tonnes).

The variation in thresholds means that in practice the number of projects subject to EIA varies enormously among Member States: a large number (c. 6000 per annum) of relatively small scale projects being caught by the net in France where low thresholds are imposed and there is wide application, whereas a small number (c. 80-100) of only major projects are subject to EIA in the Netherlands, with the UK being somewhere in between (c. 300).

The report identifies where a number of improvements should

be made. It concludes that the EIA process is, in many cases, not starting early enough, ie too often it is bolted on to the planning and design process rather than being integral from the beginning, and that there is often inadequate quality control of the environmental statement and the EIA process as a whole. Adequate mitigation measures are frequently missing from the planning and design of projects. Consultation in some cases and in some Member States is weak, and the availability of environmental statements is sometimes poor. The review also concludes that the contribution of the EIA process to decision-making and the role of monitoring project implementation are not as clear or as effective as they could be. This last point is particulary disturbing, since EIA is essentially about improving the quality of decision-making by making it more informed.

Many of the individual Member State annexes include recommendations for improving implementation in the Member State, some of which may be achieved through amending the Directive itself. One of the recommendations identified in the UK annex is that consideration should be given to the establishment of an independent statutory body to set and maintain standards relating to the EIA process. The review report has formed the basis for the Commission to bring forward proposals for amending the Directive. These amendments have been in the pipeline for some considerable time, but are now unlikely to see the light of day formally before the first quarter of 1994 after disputes among Commissioners and between Member States over the need for improvements to the Directive. The familiar (and sterile) jobs versus environment arguments are still in danger of holding sway. Also, in the light of debates over subsidiarity, it must be hoped that any amendments finally agreed by the Council will do more than merely tweak the Directive at the margins when more substantial improvements might be warranted. It is clearly important to improve the provision for and guidance on scoping and post-project monitoring, provide for better public participation and for better quality control (perhaps through a statutory agency in each Member State). Will the Commission and, more crucially, the Council be willing to see such improvements included in an amended Directive? On recent form it seems unlikely.

The amendments arising out of this review could potentially transform the Directive into a more effective tool for achieving sustainable development than hitherto. However, the review has singularly failed to address what is probably the greatest weakness of the present EIA Directive: that is, it applies only to project level decision making, thereby occurring only after crucial decisions relating to alternatives or wider environmental impacts have been taken. The report does, however, recognise this fact. This was a missed opportunity which could have helped to move forward the development of EIA as a whole in the Community. Meanwhile, proposals for a (now) simplified strategic environmental assessment (SEA) Directive creep forward in isolation from amendments to the project Directive (see Chapter 10).

EIA in North America

United States of America

Enacted in 1969, the National Environmental Policy Act (NEPA) represents the first comprehensive attempt to address environmental concerns in the decision-making of federal government agencies. While NEPA has both been praised for its pioneering, farsighted approach to environmental policy and criticized for its inefficiencies and delays, the evolving EIA procedures under NEPA have been emulated widely.

NEPA attempts to focus agencies' attention on the environmental consequences of a proposed federal action through the use of:

> "a systematic, interdisciplinary approach which will ensure the integrated use of the natural and social sciences and the environmental design arts in planning and decision-making.

NEPA accomplishes this goal by establishing a set of procedures to be followed by every federal agency before deciding to embark on a proposed activity. The most significant of these procedures is the environmental impact statement (EIS). An EIS is required for any proposal for legislation or other major federal action significantly affecting the environment. The EIS must analyze, among other things, the environmental impacts of the proposal, its alternatives, the "relationship between local, short term uses of resources and the enhancement of long-term productivity," and any irreversible commitments of resources.

In addition to the EIS requirement, NEPA established the Council on Environmental Quality (CEQ) (see Chapter 7, Enforcement) which is charged with overseeing implementation of NEPA's procedures and with promulgating regulations explaining the requirements of the Act. The NEPA regulations, published in the Code of Federal Regulations (CFR) title 40, sections 1501 to 1508, elaborate on the steps agencies must take in the EIA process.

The Regulations emphasize at the outset that the EIS is not an end itself; rather, it is a vehicle to promote environmentally sensitive decision-making. It must be concise, analytical, and cognizant of the policies of NEPA. Most importantly, the statement should be used to assess probable environmental impacts, not to justify decisions already made. In addition, since the procedures established by NEPA must be followed by every federal agency, they are meant to be amenable to a broad range of decision-making styles. Among the manifestations of this flexibility is NEPA's use of relatively broad language concerning the applicability and content of the EIS (Yost and Rubin, 1993).

When is an EIS required?

An EIS must be prepared for every proposal for legislation and other major federal actions which may significantly affect the quality of the human environment. The Regulations, generally following court decisions, elaborate on almost every word in this requirement. A "proposal" exists when an agency has a goal and is actively preparing to make a decision in furtherance of it. While such proposals must be more than mere contemplation, the EIS process must not be put off so as to delay the underlying action.

Proposals for legislation undergo different EIA procedures and are used less frequently than for agency activities, which are discussed below. The Regulations define "other major federal action" as:

> "projects and programs entirely or partly financed, assisted, conducted, regulated, or approved by federal agencies; new and revised agency rules, regulations, plans, policies, or procedures; and legislative proposals."

NEPA's application, therefore, goes beyond projects to include strategic environmental assessment (see Chapter 10).

NEPA rejects the use of a detailed list of criteria and thresholds to determine its applicability, opting instead for the broad phrase, "significantly affecting" the environment. Since, the interpretation of this term is dependent on specific facts, the necessity of an EIS is determined on a case-by-case basis, using various factors fashioned over time by the courts and reflected in the Regulations. These factors include, among others, beneficial and adverse impacts of the proposal, its likely effects on public health and safety, the unique characteristics of the geographical area, and whether the action is related to other actions with individually insignificant but cumulatively significant effects. Not surprisingly, it has been the term "significantly" which has been the subject of the majority of NEPA litigation.

Preparation of the EIS

Under NEPA it is the duty of the federal agency making the proposal to prepare the EIS. Where more than one agency is expected to have a significant role in the EIA process, the Regulations provide for the designation of a "lead agency" to assume primary responsibility for the preparation of the EIS. Where a private developer is seeking approval from a federal agency, it is the agency's responsibility to compile the EIS, although information may be submitted by the applicant.

As a result of NEPA's lack of specific thresholds or listings of proposals which require an EIS, a lead agency must first determine whether an EIS must be prepared for a certain proposal. This decision may be taken in advance through a list of categories of actions that normally do, or do not, have significant effects on the environment. (The inclusion of a particular proposal on such a list is, however, subject to judicial review.) For those categories about which a prior decision has not been made, the agency must prepare an Environmental Assessment (EA): a document which considers whether or not a particular proposal may have significant effects on the environment. An agency may permit an applicant to prepare this document, but its evaluation rests with the agency as does the responsibility for its scope and content. If the EA concludes that there will be no significant impacts on the environment, the agency may prepare a Finding of No Significant Impact (FONSI) and proceed with the planning process without an EIS. If, on the other hand, the EA finds that there may be significant impacts, steps must be taken toward preparation of an EIS.

Except for legislative proposals, EISs are most often prepared in draft and final forms. First, the lead agency along with cooperating agencies prepares a draft which is circulated to the public and to various other agencies for comments. After receiving comments from these sources, the final EIS is prepared incorporating relevant issues raised by commentators and responses to opposing views. Additionally, an EIS must be supplemented when there are substantial changes in the proposal or when new circumstances arise that would have a bearing on the environmental impacts.

Section 102 of NEPA lists the required contents of the EIS, the most important of which are the environmental impacts and alternatives. Information on environmental impacts is meant to provide the "scientific and analytical basis for the comparisons" in the alternatives section. While the Regulations set out the information that is to be included in the environmental impacts section, these requirements are flexible; and the verbose descriptions of many early EISs are specifically discouraged. The alternatives section is "the heart of the EIS," analyzing the environmental consequences of a proposal and its alternatives in comparative form. This section must discuss alternatives outside the jurisdiction of the lead agency, if any, and must always analyze the consequences of "no action."

Once the lead agency has met the content requirements and responded to public and agency comments, the final EIS must be circulated for comment in much the same manner as the draft. Furthermore, the agency is prohibited from making a decision on the proposal until 30 days after the final EIS is completed, thus allowing time for the agency to consider the information and analysis contained therein. Additionally, the agency must prepare a Record of Decision (ROD) documenting the consideration of the EIS in its decision.

California

Taking its cue from NEPA, California established an extensive system of EIA with the passage of the California Environmental Quality Act in 1970 (CEQA), implemented by the CEQA Guidelines. Currently, the Environmental Section of the State Bar of California is conducting a review of CEQA, which will result in proposals for amendments to the Act. The aim of the review is to recommend changes at both the compliance and litigation phases (a) to improve decision-making; (b) to provide greater certainty regarding the adequacy of CEQA compliance; and (c) to improve efficiency and to reduce the expense of the EIA process.

At present, the procedures of CEQA are similar to those required by NEPA. In order to determine whether EIA must be performed on a particular proposal, the lead authority performs an initial study. If the authority finds that any aspect of the proposal, either individually or cumulatively, may cause a significant adverse effect on the environment, the authority must prepare a draft environmental impact report (EIR). Conversely, if the initial study reveals that the proposal will have no significant adverse effect, a negative declaration (like NEPA's FONSI) must be prepared providing the basis for that conclusion. The draft EIR is then circulated among interested public agencies and, in most cases, put on public review at the State Clearinghouse, the agency responsible for receiving and distributing documents prepared under CEQA. After comments are received, they are incorporated into the final EIR, which is then circulated for public review.

In addition, like NEPA, CEQA requires that the decisions of public authorities address environmental concerns. No proposal may be approved under CEQA unless (a) changes in the proposal have been required to mitigate adverse effects; or (b) such changes are the responsibility of another agency; or (c) specific economic, social, or other considerations make mitigation measures or alternatives infeasible. As the latter suggests, CEQA does not require that agencies actually follow the recommendations of the EIR; rather, CEQA recognizes that EIA is essentially informational. Even so, the Guidelines require that agencies explain the reasons for their decisions. Thus, while CEQA makes broad policy declarations on the quality of the environment, its real bite is procedural.

Similar to the federal CEQ, the Office of Planning and Research, including the State Clearinghouse, provides guidance and information but not supervision, enforcement being left to the courts (see Chapter 7).

Canada

The legislative basis for EIA in Canada is in transition. In March 1992 the Federal House of Commons passed the Canadian Environmental Assessment Act (CEAA), which became effective in 1993, providing a more solid legal foundation for EIA in Canada. Before the CEAA Canadian EIA was governed by the Environmental Assessment and Review Process Guidelines

Order of 1984, which was only declared legally binding in 1989 (Canadian Wildlife Federation v Canada, (1989) 3 F.C. 309, 3 C.E.L.R. (NS.) 287, affirmed (1989) 4 C.E.L.R. (NS.) 1). The CEAA has encountered considerable opposition, however, and a brief comparison of the two structures is instructive.

Under the Guidelines Order EIA was a "self-assessment" process by which government departments were responsible for integrating environmental considerations into their own planning procedures. The department first conducted an initial assessment to determine whether the proposal may have a significant effect on the environment. If it was decided that the proposal would not have significant effects, no further steps would be necessary, and the department may make its final decision. If, however, it is determined that the proposal may have significant effects on the environment, or that public concern is great, the department must refer the proposal to an independent EIA panel for public review. The EIA Panel then studies the proposal in the light of public comments and publishes a non-binding report setting out its recommendations.

The Guidelines Order is administered by the Federal Environmental Assessment and Review Office ('FEARO'). FEARO publishes procedural guidelines for initial screenings, assists during public review, provides information to the public, and reports to the Minister of the Environment on the implementation of EIA. Nonetheless, under the Guidelines Order FEARO has not been empowered to override a departmental decision during the initial assessment or to enforce EIR content requirements.

The Guidelines Order also effectively covered policies, plans and programmes since it applied to any initiative, undertaking or activity for which the Government has a decision-making responsibility (see Chapter 10).

Several lessons can be learned from the current transition. First is the inadequacy of a system which relies on unsupervised self-assessment. Such a method carries an inherent conflict of interest, leaving departments and agencies with the exclusive responsibility for determining the nature and significance of their own proposals. The self-assessment process under the Guidelines Order has been wholly internal and hidden from public view. The CEAA may remedy this, however, by providing the Environment Minister with powers to initiate public review and to appoint mediators and intervenors.

Second, EIA procedures firmly based in statute would promote certainty. Because the Guidelines Order had not been legally binding, implementation by departments and agencies, especially in the case of SEA, was lax. The massive judicial change in the enforceability of the Guidelines Order set off a scramble by the Government to establish procedures. The CEAA should provide this foundation, but it is inadequate in other ways, most notably by restricting EIA only to projects of a "physical" nature. The CEAA would also keep SEA subject to political ebbs and flows, depriving the public of the chance to examine policies, plans, and programmes in an objective forum. Furthermore, by restricting its scope to physical projects, the CEAA misses the chance to create a consistent standard for EIA that would accompany proposals from general concept to concrete project.

Even so, due to the infancy of the CEAA, its true impact cannot yet be judged. Several vital regulations have yet to come into effect promulgated, for example, including lists of projects that will require EIA and rules for state-owned corporations. It also appears that the new Canadian Environmental Assessment Authority will expand very little on the powers of FEARO. In addition, the effectiveness of the supervisory powers of the Environment Minister has yet to be assessed.

Chapter 5

EIA IN THE UNITED KINGDOM

Introduction

The EIA Directive has been implemented in the UK through secondary legislation under section 2 (2) of the European Communities Act 1972. This has been in the form of a series of regulations implementing the Directive in a number of policy sectors where different consent procedures operate, or where there are none. The requirements of the various regulations and procedures are summarised in a booklet published by the Department of the Environment (UK DoE, 1989).

The majority of projects requiring mandatory EIA (Annex I projects) and discretionary EIA (Annex II projects) fall under the town and country planning system and generally require planning permission from local authorities. The exceptions are the major transport infrastructure projects which either require the consent of the Secretary of State for Transport or are promulgated as public, private or hybrid bills and therefore require Parliamentary approval; or projects requiring the consent of the relevant Secretary of State (which often includes deemed planning consent), such as energy projects, or projects of major significance and which are 'called-in' for determination by central Government. Although the Directive is somewhat ambiguous as to whether it applies to projects subject to Parliamentary approval, the UK Government has chosen to require EIA in such cases through amendments to Parliamentary Standing Orders (CPRE, 1991a).

While implementation under section 2(2) of the European Communities Act 1972 allows compliance with EC legislation and therefore with Directive 85/337/EEC, it provides no scope for further development of EIA within the UK beyond a strict interpretation of the requirements of the EC legislation. Regulations under s2(2) of the EC Act allow implementation only of the strict letter of the parent Directive.

To extend the scope of EIA, the benefits of which the Directive clearly signals in Article 13, primary legislation was required. In April 1991 the Government finally accepted the need for primary legislation for EIA (CPRE, 1991b) and included it in the Planning and Compensation Act 1991. Section 15 of the Act now allows the Secretary of State to make regulations for the purposes of requiring EIA for projects other than those already listed in Annex I or II of the EIA Directive. The lack of this provision had meant that certain projects slipped through the EIA net, for example drinking water treatment plants and trout farms; and the requirement for some others was at best ambiguous, for example wind farms, golf courses. These new regulations are due for publication shortly.

While strict criteria or thresholds are included in the Directive for Annex I projects, those created by the UK for Annex II are purely for guidance, and have no legal force. The use of criteria and thresholds in the determination of which projects shall be subject to EIA is a difficult issue and one which needs to be treated with considerable care. Superficially, thresholds may appear attractive offering, as the UK Government has argued, a degree of certainty to developers and authorities alike. However, thresholds should only be used where it can be guaranteed that projects falling under the threshold will not a have a significant effect on the environment. Even though thresholds used in Government guidance are indicative they are more often interpreted as being fixed (see Chapter 3).

The UK implementing regulations comprise:-

Town and Country Planning (Assessment of Environmental Effects) Regulations 1988 (SI No. 1199)

Town and Country Planning (Assessment of Environmental Effects) (Amendment) Regulations 1990 (SI No. 367) and 1992 (SI No. 1494)

Environmental Assessment (Scotland) Regulations 1988 (SI No. 1221)

Environmental Assessment (Salmon Farming in Marine Waters) Regulations 1988 (SI No.1218)

Environmental Assessment (Afforestation) Regulations 1988 (SI No. 1207)

Land Drainage Improvement Works (Assessment of Environmental Effects) Regulations 1988 (SI No. 1217)

Highways (Assessment of Environmental Effects) Regulations 1988 (SI No. 1241)

Harbour Works (Assessment of Environmental Effects) Regulations 1988 (SI No. 1336)

Harbour Works (Assessment of Environmental Effects) (No. 2) Regulations 1989 (SI No. 424)

Electricity and Pipe-line Works (Assessment of Environmental Effects) Regulations 1990 (SI No. 442)

Town and Country Planning General Development Order 1988 (SI No. 1813) (Article 14(2)) as amended

Town and Country Planning (General Development) (Scotland) Amendment Order 1988 (SI No. 977)

Town and Country Planning (General Development) (Scotland) Amendment No. 2 Order 1988 (SI No. 1249)

Similar regulations exist for Northern Ireland, although many were implemented some time after the required date of 3 July 1988.

The most important of these regulations are considered in some detail below.

Town and Country Planning (Assessment of Environmental Effects) Regulations 1988

The general tenor of the UK Government's approach to EIA has been, from the outset, grudging and minimalist. During the many years of the development of the Directive the UK Government opposed its introduction, mainly on the grounds that the long-established system of development control under town and country planning legislation was a more effective and sensitive method of assessing the environmental impacts of projects (see Chapter 2). However, many projects, including many transport, agriculture and forestry projects are not covered by such legislation. Indeed, the UK Government was instrumental in placing agricultural projects firmly in Annex II of the Directive rather than in Annex I (mandatory assessment) as favoured by some Member States (Sheate and Macrory, 1989). The UK Government had assumed, when it came to implementation, that the Annex II projects were, under Article 4(2), wholly discretionary and therefore did not require any further procedures for implementation. The UK Government eventually accepted the view of the European Commission, as required under article 11 (2) of the Directive, that criteria and/or thresholds adopted for the selection of Annex II projects should be notified to the Commission, thereby requiring suitable procedures for implementation. Even so, there are a number of areas which have still not been adequately addressed.

There is, therefore, a clear history of UK Government opposition to EIA in the first instance; both in principle and in relation to proposals that might require the establishment of a consent procedure where one did not already exist, eg agriculture (see below). The general approach has remained minimalist, in which EIA is seen as a regrettable burden on the developer which should be reduced by all means possible. This was graphically illustrated in the UK Government's pronouncement on EIA in its White Paper on the Environment published in September 1990. In it the Government said:-

> "But EIAs impose costs both on developers who are required to assemble the information and on the authorities which must evaluate it. Any case for the extension of the application of EIA must therefore be considered carefully."

The UK Government chose to incorporate the requirements of the EIA Directive, as far as possible, into the existing town and country planning system. The Government did not consider it necessary to make provision for EIA in primary legislation, but instead chose implementation by regulations - secondary legislation - under section 2 (2) of the European Communities Act 1972. Where different consent procedures exist for projects falling outside the town and country planning system, eg transport or forestry, separate regulations have been drawn up. Since this mode of implementation limits the application of the Directive strictly to the content of the Directive only, EIA could be applied only to those projects specified in the lists of Annex I and II of the Directive. Until the Planning and Compensation Act 1991 there was no scope in the UK for the wider application or refinement of the principles of the Directive.

The Government is due to publish new regulations under section 15 of the Planning and Compensation Act 1991 (section 71A of the amended Town and Country Planning Act 1990) which will extend the application of EIA to projects which currently fall outside the Directive. The publication of these regulations was much delayed during 1993 due at least in part to the Government's deregulation initiative and the difficulty in gaining the agreement of a number of Government departments.

While it can be argued that the Directive can have direct effect (the so-called doctrine of direct effect, see Chapter 9), in practice it is the implementing legislation in the Member State (in the UK, the Regulations under the European Communities Act 1972) which are the guidelines for local authorities and developers. It is therefore imperative that the implementing legislation fully implements the 'parent' Directive. If not, we see the conflicts which have been apparent in the UK.

In formulating the UK regulations the Government has chosen to employ the term 'Environmental Statement'(ES), which is not found in the EC legislation. During the lengthy drafting of the Directive there was a very real desire to avoid the problems of the US approach to EIA, by making it clear that EIA was a part of the development consent procedure and that the production of an ES was not the sole or absolute requirement. It was felt that it was the US dependency on the ES which had resulted in the weight of litigation which the EC was at pains to avoid; litigation particularly over the scope and content of the environmental statements. Developers and Member States were keen to prevent the establishment of further sources of delay in obtaining project consent (see Chapter 2).

Given that this debate had occurred it is perhaps surprising that the UK Government (and many other Member States) explicitly chose to go down this road. Indeed, it has been the poor quality of many environmental statements (acknowledged by the UK Government) which has become the focus of so much concern about EIA in the UK - precisely the issue which all were keen to avoid during the drafting of the Directive. This over-emphasis on the ES has, arguably, diverted attention from EIA as a process.

It can be argued that the UK Regulations which implement the Directive downgrade the requirements of Annex III of the Directive, in respect of information to be provided by a developer as part of an EIA. Article 5 (1) of the Directive provides the necessary discretion as far as Annex III is concerned. It can be argued that the UK Regulations provide the developer with the discretion and not the competent authority. In so doing it would appear that the UK has exercised its own (Member State) discretion under article 5 (1) by giving the developer the discretion to decide whether much of the information referred to in Annex III of the Directive be submitted to the competent authority.

The UK Regulations, where they refer to the information required by the EIA, relegate much of the Annex III requirements to little more than optional extras. Annex III lists the information required while Schedule 3 of the Town and Country Planning Regulations 1988 employs the word 'may' when referring to the provision of certain information other than that 'specified'.

Under Schedule 3 of the Town and Country Planning Regulations the 'specified' information is:

a) description of development proposed;

b) data necessary to identify and assess main effects on the environment;

c) description of likely significant effects, direct and indirect, on the environment;

d) mitigation measures;

e) a non-technical summary of the above.

Other aspects of Annex III such as forecasting methods used, alternatives studied, secondary and cumulative effects remain discretionary on the developer rather than the Member State, and are frequently left out by developers who are able to justify such omissions by referring to the regulations and Government guidelines.

While the Directive refers to consideration of alternatives "where appropriate" under Annex III arguably there may still be a requirement if it can be said to be appropriate. Under the UK regulations the developer has total discretion, whether or not it is appropriate, to provide such information or not. Indeed, on this specific point, the regulations refer to information on:

> "(in outline) the main alternatives (if any) studied by the applicant..."(Schedule 3 (3)(d)).

This implies that the developer need only consider alternatives to the proposed project if the developer thinks it is appropriate, and then only in outline. Ideally, an assessment of alternatives should be provided as part of the 'specified' information unless that is deemed inappropriate by the competent authority.

The fact that the developer does not have to justify the forecasting and assessment methods employed under UK regulations is of considerable concern. Claims may be made in an environmental statement which cannot be substantiated, yet there is no requirement for such methods to be specified. While competent authorities can require further information from a developer, the onus should be on the developer to provide the necessary information in the first place, and not require prompting by the competent authority.

The use of natural resources, the emission of pollutants, the consideration of alternatives, the likely direct, indirect, secondary, cumulative, short, medium and long term, permanent, temporary, positive and negative effects should be addressed as a matter of course unless it is inappropriate to do so. Best practice suggests that it is rarely inappropriate to consider alternatives. It would not seem unreasonable that the onus should be on the developer to address all the 'optional' implications of Schedule 3 (3) unless there is a clear reason why not, rather than an assumption that those aspects will not be addressed unless the developer considers it is relevant or is subsequently required to provide additional information. The former approach is more likely to secure consistency across authorities since an authority would need actively to delete requirements where not appropriate rather than require additional information after the submission of the ES. It would also encourage developers to consult local authorities on whether an EIA is necessary (see Chapter 6) and on its scope.

An appropriate form of words for the beginning of Schedule 3 (3) might be:-

"3. An environmental statement should, unless indicated otherwise by the competent authority, include information on the following matters:-...."

Whether certain information should be included in the ES or not will depend on whether it is deemed appropriate by the competent authority, and ultimately by the courts in the same way as 'significance' of effects.

Infrastructure and Other Projects

Under Schedule 2 (10) and (11) of the Town and Country Planning EIA Regulations a range of infrastructure and other projects can be subject to EIA where the relevant authority considers it necessary. These categories include local authority consent powers for local highways and airports.

Circular 15/88 which accompanies the Regulations suggests, for 'other' infrastructure projects, that projects requiring sites in excess of 100 ha may require EA. This guidance threshold seems to be set at a remarkably high level. Many of the projects listed in Schedule 2 (10) and (11) could have significant effects on the environment whilst occupying a considerably smaller area than 100 ha.

Agriculture

Agriculture was a central issue of controversy during the development of the EIA Directive. It was one area for which there was considerable pressure during the drafting process to require mandatory EIAs and therefore for agriculture to be included in Annex I. In part due to UK Government pressure, agriculture was finally placed in Annex II. As already described the UK was initially under the impression that it would not have to implement EIA for Annex II projects, but once forced to has found agriculture a particularly troublesome area. In the UK, agriculture is now the least well implemented of all the policy sectors covered by the EIA Directive.

The UK Government's approach to the agricultural projects included under Annex II (1) of the Directive has largely been 'do-nothing' (see Sheate and Macrory, 1989). While salmon farming in marine waters, land drainage and forestry are covered by separate regulations (see below) there are no existing consent procedures or EIA requirements for the remaining agricultural categories: the cultivation of semi-natural or uncultivated land, land reclamation from the sea, and the re-structuring of rural land holdings. The latter two classes of project are not generally seen to be relevant to the UK - the re-structuring of rural land holdings being of particular importance to France (remembrement). While there is little land reclamation from the sea at present in the UK provision for applying EIA to such projects should be made in case they assume greater importance in future as a result of climate change and rising sea levels. The cultivation for intensive agriculture of uncultivated or semi-natural land is, however, a problem in the UK, particularly with respect to moorlands, heathlands, hay meadows and wetlands. This form of cultivation is considered to be an agricultural operation and therefore permitted development, even though the development may constitute a major land use and landscape change. In the absence of any notification or consent procedure, the UK Government has found it impossible to implement the Directive for such activities.

Elsewhere, the relationship of agricultural development to the planning system has governed the EIA provisions. Many forms of agricultural development involving construction, such as some buildings and farm roads, or excavation such as ponds for fish farming, are excluded from direct consent procedures under the planning system by the General Development Order, 1988. This has caused its own problems for implementation (see below).

The Government has therefore taken a laissez-faire approach and done the minimum required to catch the largest and most obviously damaging projects. The rest are not determined according to environmental impact, but according to the availability of existing procedures. Arguments that changes in EC policy elsewhere, eg the Common Agricultural Policy (CAP), will render EIA for these projects unnecessary, ie that there will no longer be pressure for cultivating marginal land, and that policies such as set-aside result in marginal land being taken out of production, do not hold water. Changes in general policy do not necessarily prevent serious environmental damage from individual projects where other incentives or pressures may be operating. In any case, changes in such policy areas may occur and appropriate EIA procedures should already be in place.

Following action by the European Commission the UK is currently revising implementation of EIA for agriculture and forestry, including how to establish more appropriate consent procedures.

The General Development Order 1988

In March 1993 the Government published a consultation paper on its proposals to remove permitted development rights for those categories of development which, if they were not permitted development, would (a) require EIA under the Town and Country Planning EIA Regulations and (b) be likely to have a significant effect in a Special Protection Area (SPA) under the Birds Directive (79/409/EEC) or a Special Area of Conservation (SAC) under the Habitats Directive (92/43/EEC).

However, the Government's proposals take a minimalist approach which depends, as might be expected, rather too much on indicative thresholds as a guide to the need for an EIA, instead of applying broad criteria. Neither are there any proposals to withdraw permitted development rights altogether for some projects in Parts 13-17 of Schedule 2 of the GDO despite the recognition that they might have significant effects on the environment. There is no requirement in the proposals to publicise an application for a lawful development certificate - the method favoured by the Government for removing permitted development rights - and place it on the public register.

The Government argued, sensibly, that withdrawing permitted development rights (PDRs) wholesale for particular types of permitted development where it might appear to conflict with one of the Directives might risk missing some projects which might potentially breach one or other of the Directives. That would create an unfortunate loophole if that was the only approach taken. However, there is no good argument why some categories of projects should not be withdrawn wholesale from the GDO and that the system suggested by the Government should not be implemented for any other projects likely to have significant effects. In particular, many projects falling within Parts 13-17 of Schedule 2 of the GDO should be prime candidates for removing PDRs entirely, eg waste water treatment plants, local authority roads, construction of harbours or marinas. The very fact that they were identified by the consultation paper indicates the possibility of such projects having such significant effects that they require an EIA. This suggests that a larger number of projects should at least be under direct planning control with the opportunity for public scrutiny of planning applications.

The lawful development certification procedure under section 10 of the Planning and Compensation Act 1991 would appear to be an appropriate mechanism for determining whether what would otherwise be permitted development requires a planning application and an environmental impact assessment. This would involve a developer applying to a local planning authority for a lawful development certificate, to establish whether a proposed development requires planning permission. Where a certificate is refused, ie a planning application is required, there is a right of appeal to the Secretary of State. The consultation paper was, however, unclear what requirements there will be for publicity or inclusion on public registers.

By adopting both approaches - withdrawal of some PDRs wholesale and the application of the significance test to others, using the lawful development certification procedure those projects most likely to be damaging to the environment would in future require planning permission as a matter of course and could be subject to EIA in the normal way, whereas those which are less likely to, but may still have significant effects can still be subject to EIA where circumstances require it. This approach would leave the discretion as to when to require EIA with the local authority, subject to the test of significance.

Chapter 6 addresses the problem where developers fail to ask local authorities for a direction on whether EIA is required and go ahead and carry out an EIA without anyone knowing they are doing so. In these circumstances, there is little opportunity to have an input to the EIA process before the application is made. If they ask for a direction the outcome must be placed on the public register. A similar situation may occur under the system proposed in the consultation paper. There appears to be no disincentive for a developer not to seek a determination as to whether a planning application and EIA is required. By withdrawing some categories of project from PDRs altogether and placing them under direct planning control the Government would at least be able to minimise the extent to which the lawful development certification procedures could be abused by developers proceeding with the development without seeking determination from the local authority first. Appropriate guidance for the general public would also help in securing compliance with the proposed procedures.

The approach to withdrawing PDRs as laid out in the consultation paper is, however, a welcome recognition that the test of significance should be the ultimate test in requiring EIA. Which individual PD projects will require EIA, and therefore a planning application, will be left to the discretion of the local authority (with a right of appeal by the developer to the Secretary of State). However, the consultation paper proposed, in line with the Government's general approach (see Chapter 3), indicative thresholds for determining when certain permitted development projects are likely to require EIA and therefore planning permission.

The thresholds suggested in the consultation paper appear to be entirely arbitrary, eg 15 km or more for a long distance aqueduct. Furthermore the distance of 10 km for local authority road permitted development is decidedly high, as it is as an indicative threshold for roads generally. On a more general point, the designated areas often appear to be considered in the consultation paper as equivalents as far as thresholds are concerned. Yet a 1km road in a small SSSI may well have rather different impacts to a 1 km road in a National Park. This further emphasises the arbitrary nature of such thresholds, especially as differences between SSSIs and National Parks have been recognised for long distance aqueducts (all projects and those of 1 km or more respectively) and land reclamation from the sea (all projects and 0.2 ha or more respectively). Where the Government insists on using indicative thresholds, however, one would hope that, at the very least, the indicative nature of those thresholds will be stressed very clearly.

Simplified Planning Zones (SPZs) and Enterprise Zones (EZs)

Department of the Environment Circular 24/88 provides advice on the application of EIA in SPZs and EZs. For Schedule 1 projects the situation is unambiguous. Such projects must be excluded from all SPZ permissions. Two alternative approaches are possible with respect to Schedule 2 projects.

Where an SPZ scheme prescribes the particular type of development permitted it will be possible for authorities to define the permission in such a way that it excludes any project requiring EIA. In other cases, the schemes could have the effect of granting permission for Schedule 2-type developments but a developer would not be free to undertake that development without first consulting the local planning authority so that the need for EIA can be considered. Circular 24/88 suggests that, given the scope and purpose of SPZs and the nature of the areas where they are designated, there would be very few cases in which EIA would be required.

Circular 24/88 makes it clear that should new EZs be designated they would have to make provisions for EIA of projects within the scope of Annexes I and II of the EIA Directive. At the time of publication of the Circular all the EZs designate in England and Wales had occured before the Directive had come into force and so no changes were necessary to existing EZs.

Highways Regulations

Under the EC Directive EIA is always required for certain projects (Annex I), such as motorways, and may be required where a project is likely to have significant effects for a long list of other project categories (Annex II), such as local roads. The relevant regulations which relate to highways are:-

Highways (Assessment of Environmental Effects) Regulations 1988 (Statutory Instrument (SI) No. 1241)

Town and Country Planning (Assessment of Environmental Effects) Regulations 1988 (SI No. 1199)

Town and Country Planning General Development Order 1988 (SI No. 1813), Article 14(2)

The Highways Regulations are the key regulations for trunk roads and motorways, since they amend the 1980 Highways Act under which such roads are given consent. The irony of this situation should not be forgotten when dealing with EIA for trunk roads and motorway proposals: such schemes are proposed by the Department of Transport, who also carry out the environmental impact assessment and give consent to proceed with building the scheme. At no stage can there be said to be rigorous independent scrutiny. A similar situation may exist with local highway schemes proposed by local authorities, although in some cases at least the proponent will be the Local Highways Department and the consenting 'authority' the Planning Department of the same authority or the Secretaries of State for the Environment and Transport.

The New Roads & Streetworks Act 1991 now requires mandatory EIA for all private road schemes eg toll motorways. This is also expected to be implemented for local highway schemes by regulations drawn up under s.15 of the Planning and Compensation Act 1991. This places private sector road schemes into Schedule 1 of the EIA regulations. Private road proposals, alone in this field, must be submitted for consent to an authority which is not also the promoter, ie either to the Secretary of State for Transport or the local highway authority for 'toll orders' to be made or confirmed.

Trunk roads and motorways

The types of road schemes that require EIA under the provisions of the Directive and the Highways Regulations were, until July 1993, outlined in guidance given by the Department of Transport in the Departmental Standard HD 18/88, along with guidelines on the composition of Environmental Statements to be published with draft Orders. This guidance is still relevant to those schemes already under way. The new guidance will apply to new entries to the Roads Programme. The earlier guidance lists the following road construction projects as requiring EIA:-

- all new motorways and roads reserved for automobile traffic accessible from interchanges or controlled junctions and on which, in particular, stopping and parking are prohibited;

- all new trunk roads over 10km in length

- other new trunk roads over 1km in length which pass

a) through or within 100m of

i) a National Park

ii) a Site of Special Scientific Interest (SSSI) notified under s.28 of the Wildlife and Countryside Act 1981 or subject to an Order under s.2

iii) a conservation area within the meaning of the Planning (Listed Buildings and Conservation Areas) Act 1990

iv) a nature reserve within the meaning of the National Parks and Access to the Countryside Act 1949

b) through an urban area where 1500 or more dwellings lie within 100m of the centre line of the proposed road

- motorway and other trunk road improvements which are likely to have a significant effect on the environment.

The last category above means that any motorway or trunk road improvement scheme (including eg motorway widening) can be subject to EIA if it can be shown that it is likely to have a significant effect on the environment. Ultimately, of course, the test of significance is one for the courts to rule upon or the European Court via a complaint to the European Commission.

There has been some unfortunate confusion with terminology in the field of EIA and road schemes. The DOT traditionally referred to its form of environmental impact assessment as 'Environmental Appraisal' and the main guidance to carrying out such appraisal was until July 1993 the DOT's Manual of Environmental Appraisal. One of the general criticisms of the DOT's Environmental Appraisal process is that it is not iterative in the way which EIA should be, ie appraisal tends to occur at the end of the design process rather than in parallel to it, the latter enabling changes to be made in response to problems identified along the way.

The DOT's Manual of Environmental Appraisal (MEA), along with the Departmental Standard HD 18/88 set out the formal appraisal procedure which attempted to reconcile technical requirements with economic considerations and environmental effects. The MEA was introduced in 1983 and went through a revision process in the early 1990s. The revised manual was published as Volume 11 of the DOT's Design Manual for Roads and Bridges (Environmental Assessment) and brings a number of significant improvements to the language used by the DOT, including the need for EIA to be iterative. The term 'environmental appraisal' has finally been replaced by 'environmental assessment'. The Highways regulations, however, remain unamended.

The central component of the old MEA was the use of a tabulated summary - the 'framework' - that considered the effects of the proposed road scheme on six different receptor groups.

These groups were:-

    travellers

    occupiers of property

    users of facilities

    policies for conserving and enhancing the area

    policies for development and transport

    financial effects

The limitations of this approach are evident since the consideration of environmental effects was limited to the effect of the proposed scheme on 'policies' for conservation and enhancement and tended to exclude wider environmental issues. The framework was also heavily biased towards user groups, ie people who are more likely to benefit from a road scheme even if only marginally, for instance in terms of time savings on journeys, rather than wider environmental parameters. The new Manual retains a similar framework (referred to as Environmental Impact Tables or EITs) which now cover the following categories:-

A: Appraisal groups

    1.   Local people and their Communities

2. Travellers

3. The Cultural and Natural Environment

4. Policies and Plans

B: Land Use Table

C: Mitigation Table

Cost Benefit (COBA) and financial effects have been removed from the new EITs. A cynic might suggest that this is a deliberate attempt to camouflage the importance that COBA has on decision-making. The fact that COBA is now dealt with separately in formal terms does not make it any less important.

An 'environmental appraisal/assessment' is carried out for all road schemes promoted by DOT. However, the documentation is only published as an Environmental Statement (ES) when the criteria laid down in the Departmental Standard HD18/88 are satisfied. An ES must also include a non-technical summary published either as part of the ES or, preferably, separately. Even where an ES is not published the details of the appraisal should be available at a public inquiry.

Elsewhere in the Manual there is guidance on techniques for assessing environmental impact, including noise, visual impact, air pollution, severance, ecological impact etc. Curiously little of this information has tended in the past to find its way into environmental statements. Instead, it was the framework which most often formed the core of a DOT ES. It is to be hoped that the new Manual will result in rather more informative ESs in future.

The DOT's own Standing Advisory Committee on Trunk Road Assessment (SACTRA) reported in 1992 (DOT, 1992) on the assessment methods used by the DOT and concluded that they were in need of considerable overhaul, including the need for earlier and wider assessment and consultation. At present, an Environmental Statement is produced to accompany the draft Orders for the preferred route option. There is not, however, any opportunity under the present system to consider alternatives other than different routes, eg significant traffic management schemes, even though the proper consideration of alternatives should be a central facet of EIA. This illustrates the differences between the DOT's environmental appraisal/ assessment process and EIA. The emphasis of DOT's environmental appraisal/assessment is still on mitigating damaging effects of the preferred option (usually preferred because of time savings and cost under the framework methodology and Cost Benefit Analysis (COBA)) rather than modifying the proposal or options to eliminate or minimise the likely damaging effects on the environment. The DOT therefore lays great emphasis on the numbers of trees it plants as part of its road building schemes, even though these can in no way be considered a quid pro quo for the loss, for instance, of ancient woodland or heathland. The production of the ES occurs only after the Public Consultation stage on the preferred option by which time many crucial decisions will already have been taken, not least that a road is needed at all. While the assessment process may address alternative routes (though not other different solutions) using the framework/EIT methodology, only the preferred option is usually addressed in the ES.

The new Manual has done nothing to resolve the failure of the DOT's EIA procedures to address whole routes rather than only small sections of roads (see also Chapter 10). It includes some guidance on cumulative effects of related schemes, but only suggests that early consideration is desirable. No procedure is established to enable it to happen. The other major defect is the failure to consider realistic alternatives other than alternative routes. The fact that the new Manual is Volume 11 of the Design Manual for Roads and Bridges emphasises the late stage at which EIA is being applied; the decision to build a road is taken before EIA comes into play.

Local highway schemes

Road schemes promoted by local highway authorities come under the Town and Country Planning EIA Regulations and not the Highways EIA Regulations. However, because there has been little Government guidance on carrying out EIA for road schemes other than the DOT's Manual of Environmental Appraisal and the Departmental Standard HD 18/88, most local highway authorities have followed the procedures of the MEA and Standard. The key differences are that if the DOT's methods are followed they will invariably focus on the limited framework approach without addressing direct and indirect effects of the proposal in full, as required by the Directive and the Planning EIA Regulations. Although the provision of certain information listed in Annex III of the Directive as 'information to be supplied by the developer' is at the discretion of the Member State government, the Planning EIA Regulations list this as information which may be included in an ES (Schedule 3 (3)). The Highways EIA Regulations, by contrast, leave out a large proportion of the information listed in Annex III. The Departmental Standard explicitly stated that certain information listed in Annex III, such as that regarding the use of natural resources, need not be addressed specifically in an ES. This has now been superseded by the new Manual which no longer makes specific exclusions.

Under the Planning EIA Regulations a local authority Planning Department is much more likely to ask for further information (as it is entitled to, until satisfied) from a Highways Department, including relevant aspects of the optional information categories, than the Department of Transport is to ask itself! The Highways Regulations require only the minimum of information under the Directive, without detailing additional types of information that can be supplied or might be appropriate (although Annex III is referred to its contents are not). The revised manual has made no difference to the Highways regulations which remain unamended.

Since local highway schemes go through 'normal' planning procedures, albeit deemed planning consent by the county council, ESs produced by local authorities may be more likely to address wider planning issues, including the possible implications of the scheme for consequential development attracted to the new road. There is also likely to have been more opportunity to influence early ideas for local road schemes through the structure and local plan processes so that where local highway schemes do come forward there should already have been a chance to address the question of need for the road. This is manifestly not the case with DOT promoted schemes.

Electricity and Pipe-line Works (Assessment of Environmental Effects) Regulations 1989/90

These electricity regulations appeared considerably later than those for other Departments, giving rise to uncertainty, particularly about the status of nuclear power stations which are explicitly included in Annex I of the Directive. They originally came into force on 9 February 1989, seven months later than the majority of the other regulations. New Regulations were issued as a consequence of the privatisation of the electricity industry under the Electricity Act 1989. These new Regulations came into force on 31 March 1990 (SI 442).

The Regulations cover all electricity generating stations and activities requiring consent (including deemed planning consent) from the Secretary of State for Energy (now Trade and Industry), other than those that fall under the Town and Country Planning Regulations and therefore subject to local authority control (ie power stations of less than 50 MW capacity).

Power stations

Thermal power stations with a heat output of 300MW or more and nuclear power stations fall under the mandatory requirements of Annex I of the Directive. Unfortunately, the wording in the Town and Country Planning Regulations was, when first in force, somewhat ambiguous.

Schedule 1 (2) of the original Town and Country Planning Regulations stated:-

> "A thermal power station or other combustion installation with a heat output of 300 megawatts or more, other than a nuclear power station or other nuclear reactor."

It was not clear from this whether the threshold of 300 MW applied to thermal power stations, and that all nuclear power stations or reactors should also be subject to mandatory EIA; or whether only thermal power stations greater than 300 MW required mandatory EIA, and nuclear stations did not. This undoubtedly needed clarification. As a result of the passing of the Electricity Act 1989 both the Electricity and the Town and Country Planning Regulations were amended to take account of the fact that under section 36 of the 1989 Electricity Act, proposals for generating stations below 50 MW output would fall under the normal planning regime.

The amended Electricity Regulations refer to 'generating stations' as defined in section 64 of the 1989 Electricity Act:-

> "in relation to a generating station wholly or mainly driven by water, includes all structures and works for holding or channelling water for a purpose directly related to the generation of electricity by that station."

This definition clearly includes nuclear power stations, as do the amended Town and Country Planning Regulations (SI 367, 1990):-

Paragraph (1) 2 of Schedule 1 now reads:

> "2(a) A thermal power station or other combustion installation with a heat output of 300 megawatts or more (not being an installation falling within paragraph (b)); and
>
> (b) A nuclear power station or other nuclear reactor

(excluding a research installation for the production and conversion of fissionable and fertile materials, the maximum power of which does not exceed 1 kilowatt continuous thermal load)."

It is now quite clear that nuclear power stations are covered fully by the Regulations. However, it is not altogether clear why generating stations appear in Schedule 1 of the Town and Country Planning Regulations in the first place, since the consenting authority for such projects is the Secretary of State for Trade and Industry, and the relevant regulations are the Electricity Regulations.

Overhead transmission lines

Environmental impact assessments are not generally required for overhead transmission lines of less than 10 miles in length. Yet again the problem is the absence of an appropriate consent procedure. The erection of overhead power lines less than 10 miles in length, while falling under the normal planning regime as opposed to requiring deemed consent from the Secretary of State for Trade and Industry, is defined as permitted development under the General Development Order 1988. Hence there is no effective consent procedure to which an EIA requirement can be tied without bringing development which is currently exempt into the consent procedures.

The case study of Wilton Power Station in Chapter 10 illustrates the major problems associated with EIA implementation for power transmission lines. Currently, there is no requirement that the power transmission line requirements be considered as part of the EIA for the power station. Yet the need for transmission lines from a new power station is entirely dependent on the existence of the project and therefore should be considered as part of the EIA.

It is particularly important that piecemeal assessment and consent procedures should not allow a developer to pass the responsibility of assessing all likely environmental impacts on to another company or agency, as is currently allowed under the Electricity EIA Regulations.

The Environmental Assessment (Afforestation) Regulations 1988

These regulations came into force on 15 July 1988 and again reflect the difficulties of implementing EIA in the UK where no formal consent procedure exists. The regulations, in line with the Directive, deal only with afforestation; there is no provision for EIA for tree felling (nor is this possible in the UK without either amendment of the Directive or the inclusion of forestry projects within the EIA regulations to be drawn up under section 15 of the Planning and Compensation Act 1991), or for built development within forestry operations, eg forest roads.

There is no 'consent' system for forestry projects in the UK. Instead, the Government has resorted to the existing forestry grant aid scheme as the nearest approximation to a consent procedure available. The Forestry Commission, therefore, does not have the power to incorporate EIA procedures where no grant is sought. This system is currently under review following action by the European Commission.

Article 8 of the Directive requires that the information gathered in pursuance of the Directive's requirements 'must be taken into consideration in the development consent procedure', and a development consent is defined in Article 1 to mean the decision of the competent authority or authorities 'which entitles the developer to proceed with the project'. Article 2 (2) permits the assessment procedure to be integrated into existing procedures for consent or failing this, 'into other procedures or into procedures to be established to comply with the aims of this Directive'.

Member States therefore have considerable discretion about how and where to implement the procedures, but the implication is that for a project falling within Annex I or Annex II, there must be a power of a competent authority to make a decision that 'entitles' the developer to proceed. Although 'entitles' is not defined, it is likely that the courts would interpret this to imply a power to prohibit the development. It cannot be restricted to mean solely a decision of a competent authority which may or may not assist the developer to proceed (ie by giving financial aid).

While there have been few examples of forestry proposals in recent years without grant aid it is questionable whether that justifies the limitation of EIA solely to grant aided projects. The lack of non-grant aided projects in recent years has been largely due to the removal in 1988 of tax concessions which previously encouraged widespread commercial afforestation and had led to projects proceeding without grant aid. However, it is precisely because of possible future changes in policy which makes it desirable for the EIA mechanism to be already in place, in the same way as with EIA and agriculture (Sheate and Macrory, 1989).

The Forestry Commission published its guidelines for EIA in the form of a booklet, 'Environmental Assessment of Afforestation Projects' (August 1988). There are few thresholds to indicate when a proposal is likely to be subject to EIA, each being decided on a case by case basis. EIA is, however, considered to be more likely for any new planting in a National Nature Reserve or Site of Special Scientific Interest, or in other nationally designated areas. The only occasion when an EIA must be carried out is when a proposal in a designated area is for more than 100 hectares. This threshold may imply that proposals below 100 hectares need not be subject to EIA, when in fact smaller projects may be highly damaging in sensitive locations. The threshold also only applies to designated areas.

An example of a forestry project which might have been expected to qualify for an EIA (had the regulations applied) but did not is that of the forestry scheme proposed at Glen Dye in Scotland, which is addressed in detail in Chapter 9.

There is nothing in the regulations to require the Forestry Commission to carry out the assessment procedure in relation to its own afforestation schemes. Section 1(4) of the Forestry Act 1967 gives the Minister of Agriculture, Fisheries and Food the power to issue directions to the Commissioners, and this power could be employed to require them to carry out environmental assessment procedures in relation to their own projects. So far this has not been necessary since the Forestry Commission has applied similar criteria to its own projects. However, there is no requirement in the Regulations or guidance to indicate this. It is unfortunate that a more formal statement (other than Ministerial statements in Parliament or press notices) has not been required as part of the implementing regulations. The decision of the European Court in EC Commission v Belgium (1982 CMLR 627) requires that implementation of Directives be achieved in a form that is open and not easy to change.

The Directive does not explicitly require that the competent authority is a distinct body from the proposer of the development, and envisages that a 'developer' can be a 'public authority which initiates a project' (Article 2). It is questionable whether an internal decision about whether to proceed with the proposal might amount to a decision 'which entitles the developer to proceed'. There is a strong case for arguing that the final decision in respect of a Forestry Commission proposal which requires EIA should rest with Agriculture or Environment Ministers. Indeed, the proposals concerning Land Drainage (see below) take precisely that course.

It was just this sort of difficulty over what constitutes a 'competent' authority that caused the UK Government to re-think its privatisation proposals for the water industry, and propose in July 1987 an independent regulatory authority, the National Rivers Authority. This followed a legal opinion sought by CPRE (Jacobs and Shanks, 1986) which suggested that it would be unlikely that private water companies could be regarded as 'competent' authorities in ensuring their own compliance with EC water pollution directives. While the Forestry Commission is a public authority primarily with forestry development responsibilities it also has a specific promotional role which arguably creates a conflict of interest. It is not at all clear that the Forestry Commission's status as a Government department justifies its exemption from the provisions of the regulations, or that it is an appropriate competent authority for the purposes of EIA.

The role of the Minister to make directions is central to the EIA procedures relating to forestry projects. First, an applicant for a grant may apply (appeal) to the Minister for a direction to overrule a decision of the Forestry Commissioners that environmental information is required (Regulation 6). Second, under Regulation 7 the Minister may give a direction of his own that environmental information is required where the Commissioners 'have decided to the contrary'. This protective power of the Minister is of critical importance in the light of the Commission's statutory duties to promote afforestation, and provides that the Government can ensure that the obligations under the Directive are applied to particular projects. However, there are some fundamental problems with the present drafting.

The direction to overrule the Forestry Commission can only be employed where the Commissioners 'have decided to the contrary' (ie that no environmental information is required). Under Regulation 4, a person seeking a grant may apply in advance to the Commission asking whether or not an environmental assessment will be required. Regulation 4 (5) provides that if the Forestry Commission does not give a written opinion within 4 weeks, 'it shall be presumed that in their opinion environmental information would not be required'. Could the Minister at that point use his power under Regulation 7? It is not clear whether a 'presumed' opinion of the Commission under Regulation 4 falls within the terms of Regulation 7 - ie that the Commission 'have decided to the contrary'. If there is doubt about this (which there appears in the present text), it should be remedied.

Moreover, Regulation 7 provides no time limits for the exercise of the Minister's powers. Can he use them only before an application for grant is actually made? Or could he issue a direction at any time before the final decision of the Commissioners is made?

These regulations and the way in which EIA implementation is linked to the grant aiding procedure are currently under review following EC infringement action in 1991.

The Land Drainage Improvement Works (Assessment of Environmental Effects) Regulations 1988

These regulations came into force on 16 July 1988 and apply to land drainage improvement works carried out by the National Rivers Authority, internal drainage boards, and local authorities. These cover Annex II Class 1(c) projects ('water management projects for agriculture'). In themselves, the procedures appear to fulfil the obligations under the Directive in respect of such public authority works. The authorities must publicise all proposals for improvement works, leaving the Minister (for Agriculture, Fisheries and Food in England) to decide whether the Directive applies, if representations are made to that effect and the authority does not propose to prepare a statement (Regulation 2 (b)); and where an ES is prepared, the decision to proceed with the development rests with the Minister if objections are not withdrawn (Regulation 8 (3)). These procedures avoid some of the problems associated with the Forestry Commission arrangements.

The important 'protective' role of the Minister both in relation to requiring an environmental statement and in making the final consent is conditional upon representations being made and not withdrawn (Regulations 3 (3) and 8 (3)). Unwithdrawn representations may be an indicator of likely significant impact, but it is questionable whether the overseeing power of the Minister should depend on this happening. At the very least, the Minister should have an unrestricted power to require that an ES be prepared in any particular case. It is also preferable that he should be the final arbiter in all cases.

The regulations do not apply to any drainage works or other water management projects carried out by private individuals or bodies. Unless there are convincing arguments that no water-management project for agriculture carried out by private individuals has a significant effect on the environment, it appears that these regulations do not fully implement the obligations under the Directive with respect to such works.

The Environmental Assessment (Salmon Farming in Marine Waters) Regulations 1988

These regulations came into force on 15 July 1988 and apply to applications for consent for salmon farming in marine waters to the Crown Estate Commissioners. These regulations apply only to Scotland. While the regulations are made under the European Communities Act 1972 by the Secretary of State for Scotland the consent procedure is entirely under the jurisdiction of the Crown Estate Commissioners (CEC). There is no provision in the Regulations for the Secretary of State for Scotland to intervene. The CEC have set a threshold of 6,000 or 12,000 square metres depending on locality. Apart from the fact that surface area alone is a questionable criterion to use, these thresholds effectively exclude almost all marine fish farm developments from the need for assessment.

There has been considerable disquiet over the implementation of these regulations in Scotland. The limited application of EIA to Annex II (1) (g) projects in Scotland presumes that there is no salmon breeding outside Scotland in the UK, which may or may not always be true in the future. It has also been anomalous that only salmon farming is covered in the English version of the Directive. This was the consequence of a mistranslation from the French - it should have referred to salmonids (the salmon family) which includes trout and char. The UK Government clearly took advantage of the limitations of implementation under s2(2) of the European Communities Act 1972. Had the Directive been implemented originally under primary legislation in the UK EIA could have been applied more widely to fish farming, including inland trout farming as intended, without great difficulty. This can now been remedied by the regulations under section 15 of the Planning and Compensation Act 1991 (see above).

The Harbour Works (Assessment of Environmental Effects) Regulations 1988

These regulations came into force on 3 August 1988 and relate to requirements for EIA to accompany an application for a harbour revision order or harbour empowerment orders made to the Minister of Agriculture, Fisheries and Food or to the Secretary of State for Transport. The Regulations amend the Harbours Act 1964. The relevant Minister decides whether an EIA is needed. Where EIA is required an environmental statement must be submitted in accordance with Annex III of the Directive to the extent that the Secretary of State considers it relevant and that the applicant may reasonably be required to provide the information.

Transport and Works Rules 1992

In addition to the regulations outlined above, since 1 January 1993 new rail, light rail and guided transport systems are subject to EIA in accordance with the Transport and Works (Applications and Objections Procedure) Rules 1992 (SI No. 2902) made under the Transport and Works Act 1992.

Chapter 6

PUBLIC PARTICIPATION

Introduction

A first glance at the EC Directive on EIA (85/337/EEC) might suggest that the earliest opportunity for public participation in the environmental impact assessment process is on the publication of the information supplied to the competent authority (the 'environmental statement' in the UK). While that may be the true letter of the law it would be to misunderstand totally the purpose and process of EIA.

The principle underlying EIA generally is to consider the environmental effects of a proposal - be it project, plan, programme or policy - at the earliest possible opportunity in the planning process:-

> "....whereas they [EC Member States] affirm the need to take effects on the environment into account at the earliest possible stage in all the technical planning and decision-making processes..."
>
> Preamble to EC Directive 85/337/EEC

Such an objective cannot realistically be achieved without first consulting those people who are most likely to be affected by a particular proposal. They will be the people who know their own local environment and will be able to identify key areas of concern. Those concerns and fears may, in some cases, prove to be ill-founded, but if they are not identified at the earliest possible opportunity, they may arise at a much later stage when they are more likely to lead to conflict. By involving the public as early as possible issues may be identified which 'experts' might not have considered important, but which could prove to have a degree of importance out of all proportion to the magnitude of the impact.

So, while legislation may lay down minimum requirements for public consultation, particularly in relation to the documentation stage - in the UK, the 'environmental statement' (ES) - no developer or authority should consider that that degree of consultation alone is sufficient. If they do they may be in for a rude awakening: nothing irritates the public more than proposals which are sprung on them, with the first anyone knowing about a proposal being when a planning application is made and an environmental statement is published.

Public consultation in the UK

In the UK, the implementing regulations provide for public participation and for access to information in a variety of ways. The provisions are not, however, entirely consistent between one set of regulations and another. The majority of projects fall under the Town and Country Planning (Assessment of Environmental Effects) Regulations 1988 and these are described in some detail below.

The first indication the public may get that a developer is required to submit an environmental statement with a planning application is if the developer has made a formal request to the local planning authority for an opinion on the need for EIA. If so, the planning authority must give its opinion within three weeks of being requested and place its opinion upon the public register. Developers may appeal to the Secretary of State should they disagree with the opinion of the local planning authority, with the same period of time applying. This procedure means that the public may be made aware that an EIA will be carried out some considerable time before an ES is published; for major projects this may be months or years beforehand.

However, there is a fundamental flaw in this procedure and that is that most developers do not make formal requests to local planning authorities as to whether an EIA is required. They simply look at the schedules of the regulations, decide that one is likely to be required and proceed with it. The consequence is that no opinion is placed on the public register, the public therefore being none the wiser until a much later date. This situation is especially likely to be the case for major projects since developers are now likely to produce an EIA as a matter of course in such cases.

The next formal opportunity for public consultation is when an environmental statement is published. The developer must publish notices in the press and post site notices indicating where an environmental statement may be inspected and how copies may be obtained. Developers may make a 'reasonable' charge for ESs, though the Department of the Environment appears unable or unwilling to take sanctions against developers who charge £80, £100 or up to £300 for full environmental statements. To date there has been no case law to test what is a reasonable charge; hardly surprising, given the costs involved in taking such a case before judicial review. Under the EC Directive (see Appendix 1) and the UK Regulations a non-technical summary must also be produced as an aid to public consultation, though there is no regulation to insist that it be published separately, nor that it should be free.

Having published the environmental statement there follows a period of 21 days for inspection by the public before the ES is submitted with the planning application. Once the application is officially received by the planning authority the authority has 16 weeks (twice the period for an application not accompanied by an ES) to determined its decision on the application, unless extended by the mutual consent of the applicant. Representations must be made by the public and third parties within 21 days of the application being received. If the information received is deemed by the competent authority to be inadequate it may request further information until it is satisfied that sufficient information has been provided to enable it to evaluate the likely significant environmental effects of the proposal. The Government intends to amend the regulations to require such supplementary information to be published and subject to public consultation in the same way as the original ES. In practice, this happens in a large number of such cases already since it is in both the developer's and the local authority's interest that the public be consulted adequately.

The planning authority must then consider the application with the environmental statement and representations made by the public and statutory consultees. The decision period must not be less than 21 days, the content of the decision being made public and any conditions attached.

Following infringement action by the European Commission in October 1991 (see Chapter 9), the UK Government agreed to amend the regulations to require a written statement to be made which indicates that all necessary information and submissions have been provided to the competent authority and assessed in accordance with article 3 of the Directive. Publication of the amended regulations is still awaited, the current regulations simply requiring the information provided by the developer and the representations made by the public and others to be taken into account in the decision making process. The Commission's view is that this is inadequate since there must be evidence that an assessment of the information provided has been made, even if the developer's information may include a degree of assessment.

Projects not falling under the planning EIA regulations are, in some cases subject to rather different time periods for public consultation and decision making. For example, the regulations governing time scales for approval of power stations, transmission lines and pipelines - the Electricity (Application for Consent) Regulations 1990 - allow a maximum time of 8 weeks for local authorities to comment on an application to the Secretary of State for deemed planning consent. This is somewhat anomalous and contrasts with the situation for normal planning applications accompanied by an ES where local authorities have 16 weeks in which to come to a decision. There has been no attempt by the Government to amend this, even though this issue received a high profile in the lead up to one of the most controversial of recent power line cases, that of the North Yorkshire Power Lines Inquiry in 1992.

Public participation and consultation in the rest of the EC

Other EC Member States have implemented broadly similar measures, or adapted existing procedures, for public consultation so that the public is given an opportunity to comment on the environmental information at the time or soon after it is submitted to the competent authority, and generally before a decision is reached (CEC, 1993). In the Netherlands, detailed provision is made for public consultation at two stages in the process: first, at the establishment of the EIA guidelines (scoping) and second, when the EIS is evaluated. A public hearing takes place at this second stage with no restrictions on 'the public concerned'. Ireland unusually has provision for right of appeal to the national planning board by third parties. Belgium on the other hand has contrasting arrangements for public participation in Wallonia and Flanders. In Wallonia there is public involvement in the scoping procedure and arrangements for public hearings before decisions are taken. This contrasts markedly with Flanders where consultation of the public does not occur until after the environmental statement has been certified as complying with the legal requirements by the competent authority (Sheate & Cerny, 1993).

The European Community is now in the process of further pursuing the principles underlying the EIA Directive, albeit very slowly. As we have seen (Chapter 2) it has always been its intention that EIA of projects was the first step, while being the only step at the time which could be justified under the Treaty of Rome. The Single European Act (and the Maastricht Treaty) now means that environmental legislation has a legitimacy of its own which it did not have previously, and therefore makes it legally possible to proceed with the next stage of EIA - the application of EIA to strategic decision making. This is crucial to the future credibility of EIA, not only because it means that the environmental effects of such proposals will be considered much earlier (see Part III), but also because of the earlier opportunities it presents for the public to have access to information and to feel that they have an input into the planning and decision-making process. The denial of access to information and the feeling of powerlessness engendered by decisions delivered with minimal public participation creates frustration and anger among the general public that the system - far from working to the benefit of society as a whole - is working against them, and that their views are irrelevant or will simply be ignored. Nowhere has this been better exemplified in the UK than in relation to road proposals, where the competent authority is also the proponent, be it the Department of Transport for trunk roads and motorways or in some cases the local highways authority for local roads. The lack of independent scrutiny of such proposals has further heightened the conflict between road proponents and the public (see Chapter 7).

Improving public participation

Environmental impact assessments often fall short of the ideal because of a lack of attention to the 'scoping' process, ie the way in which the parameters of the EIA are determined. This should include the identification of the various national, regional and local policies, and indeed international obligations, within which the proposal should be seen. It should also determine the relevant alternatives, be they alternative projects, processes or options, which will need to be addressed by the EIA. The public has a vital role to play in this scoping process and a good environmental statement (ES) will indicate the ways in which the public have been involved. The case study below illustrates the way in which the public can play a constructive role throughout the whole of the EIA process. In this way the public can <u>participate</u> in the process, not simply be <u>consulted</u> on its outcome.

Case Study: Broad Oak Reservoir

More recently we have begun to see some developers and consultants recognising the value of early consultation and adequate scoping. The example of the Broad Oak Reservoir proposal in Kent is instructive and illustrates the value of publishing a scoping document at the earliest opportunity (Binnie and Partners, 1991a). It identified the key issues to be addressed and invited comments as to whether the scope as identified was adequate. The scope of the early environmental impact assessment quite properly widened to encompass the range of options and potential impacts of meeting the objective of supplying water in Kent. This included options other than just supply options, particularly those of demand management. This scoping document was followed six months later by an 'Issues and Options' document (Binnie and Partners, 1991b) which provided an assessment of the relative merits, costs and impacts of the various options and combinations of options. After a further period of consultation the Steering Committee of the water companies decided to pursue the reservoir option (and other supply options), though rejected the view of many consultees of addressing demand management first.

Unfortunately having decided to press ahead with the reservoir proposal the 'Terms of Reference' document (for the ES itself), published almost a year after the initial scoping document, was not distributed to consultees in the same open way as the previous documents. The effect on consultees was noticeable, not so much because of the decision to press ahead with the reservoir, but because the latest documentation had been given such a restricted circulation. The willingness to consult appeared to have evaporated. However, the early consultation process occurred prior to the production of any ES, addressed the majority of key issues and was constructive and relatively conflict-free. Had the process been followed through fully, the decision over which options would have been most appropriate might have been rather different. Indeed, as far as many were concerned, the EIA process had clearly identified demand management as the way forward in the first instance, rather than immediate new sources of supply. There has as yet been no planning application for the reservoir, not least because the views of some of the water companies involved has changed as demand has failed to rise as fast as projected, and the national debate over water resources and demand management continues apace.

This example also illustrates how what started out as a project became a much more strategic plan once effective scoping had been carried out, illustrating the difficulties of identifying the boundaries between projects, programmes, plans and policies, but also the need for EIA at earlier decision levels. Ultimately, the success or otherwise of early consultation as part of a broad EIA depends on the willingness of the developer to see EIA and all that it entails as a positive process for identifying the most environmentally sensitive way of meeting the objectives. If it is seen as purely a public relations exercise to justify decisions already taken it will soon become apparent to all concerned.

Freedom of access to environmental information

More recently than the EIA Directive, The EC Directive on Freedom of Access to Environmental Information (90/313/EEC) was adopted on 23 May 1990, coming into force at the end of 1992, and provides for public authorities in Member States who hold information on the environment to make it available to anyone requesting it, subject to certain exclusions. Public authorities must respond to a request for information within two months, but may refuse to provide it, stating their reasons, where it affects:

-confidentiality of the proceedings of public authorities, international relations or national defence,

-public security,

-matters which are sub judice,

-commercial and industrial confidentiality,

-confidentiality of personal data and/or files,

-material supplied by a third party without that party being under a legal obligation to do so,

-material which if disclosed would increase the likelihood of damage to the environment.

A request may also be refused if it would involve supplying unfinished documents or data or internal communications or where it is "manifestly unreasonable or formulated in too general a manner".

The Directive is implemented in the UK partly by the public registers kept by some regulatory authorities, eg planning registers, discharge and abstraction registers, integrated pollution control registers. Provisions have been made for access to other information through the Environmental Information Regulations 1992 (SI No. 3240).

This Directive provides an additional safeguard for the public in gaining access to certain information and might provide another lever in securing infringement action against a Member State which failed to implement the requirements for provision of information to the public under the EIA Directive. It might also be used as a lever for eliciting EIA information from competent authorities. For example, should a developer charge say £150 for an ES, arguably under the Freedom of Access to Information Directive one might be able to request a copy of the ES from the competent authority at a 'reasonable cost' which might, for instance, be regarded as the cost of photocopying.

Outside Europe

United States

It is interesting to contrast the approach to public involvement taken in some European countries with that of the US where the public is consulted on a draft EIS and the final EIS.

In the case of Laurel Heights Improvement Association of San Francisco, Inc. v. The Regents of the University of California, C.A. Ist, Nos. A052852 and A052853, May 12, 1992, the Court of Appeal concluded that the purpose of an Environmental Impact Report (EIR) under the California Environmental

Quality Act (CEQA) was to warn the public and officials of changes in the environment before they reached an irreversible stage and that public participation is key to the EIR process.

A draft EIR was prepared for the proposed relocation of the University of California at San Francisco's School of Pharmacy's biomedical research facilities to the Laurel Heights district. It disclosed the use of possibly radioactive, toxic and carcinogenic substances at the site. In a prior case in which the Laurel Heights Improvements Association of San Francisco Inc. challenged the Regents of the University of California's compliance with CEQA, the California Supreme Court directed the Regents to prepare a new EIR due to insufficient description of the project and inadequate discussions of feasible alternatives to the project.

A new, more thorough EIR was produced by the Regents. After the draft EIR was published and public comment solicited, the Regents published a final EIR and certified it as complying with CEQA. Laurel Heights contended that the final EIR contained significant new information which required the Regents to re-circulate the final EIR for additional public comment. The trial court denied Laurel Heights request for writ of mandate. The Court of Appeal, however, reversed this decision. The Public Resources Code Section 21092.1 provides that when significant new information is added to an EIR after public comment on it has been completed, the final EIR must be published for additional public comments. Re-circulation is not required when the revision clarifies or adds insignificant modifications to an already adequate EIR. In this case the final EIR contained additional studies on the effects of noise generated by the project on the Laurel Heights area containing measurements made after the draft EIR had been completed. The final EIR showed that the wrong standard for acceptable noise levels had been used in the draft EIR. The final EIR also contained a new experimental study on the potential cumulative toxic air impact from all sources in the Laurel Heights area which, although it demonstrated no new adverse environmental impact, the court concluded was significant enough to be revealed and commented on by the public.

An example of best practice in public participation in the US is shown below.

Case Study: Domenigoni Reservoir

The value of involving the public at the earliest opportunity is well illustrated by the example of the proposed Domenigoni Reservoir in Southern California (Gorman, 1993). This proposal involves the creation of a reservoir 250 feet deep with a surface area of 4,410 acres. The reservoir itself would be 4.5 miles long and 2 miles wide. The construction of the reservoir will require three earth dams: one 1.8 miles long, 280 feet high; another 2.2 miles long, 178 feet high; and a smaller dam to close a northern ridgeline gap. The total cost of the project is $2.25 billion including new water pipelines. The area to be flooded is largely farmland, but includes prehistoric and historic American Indian (Luiseno and Cahuilla) village sites and habitats of the endangered Stephens kangaroo rat and gnatcatcher songbird.

Remarkably the proposal has been approved with very little dissent from environmentalists or Native American Indians because of the way in which the proponent - Southern California's water agency, Metropolitan Water District (MWD), involved all interests from the beginning. The Domenigoni Valley site was chosen because the land had been farmed for more than 100 years and was therefore considered to be environmentally disturbed; an aqueduct passes through the site, so the mechanism to fill the lake was already in place; and there was ample land nearby to set aside as nature reserves, to offset the loss of habitat in the valley. The water agency purchased some 3,500 acres of land on the Santa Rosa Plateau, west of Murietta several miles away at a cost of $15.4 million. This land, adjacent to a state nature reserve, was otherwise destined for residential development. A further $1.7 million was provided for a trust fund to help manage the site, one of the largest undisturbed sites of Californian native grassland and coastal and Engelmann oaks. This purchase was regarded as mitigating the loss of the Valley's pastureland. The water agency, MWD, next bought 2,400 acres just across the southern ridgeline of the reservoir site specifically as habitat for the endangered Stephens kangaroo rat. This site already hosts a healthy kangaroo rat population, but its purchase has ensured its future survival. The final hurdle for the water company was the gnatcatcher songbird. Ten pairs were captured and released in the hills above the valley and 9,000 acres of land around the reservoir have been set aside as a nature reserve for the gnatcatcher and 16 other sensitive bird, animal and plant species. As a result, environmental groups and the US Department of Fish and Wildlife gave the thumbs up to this project.

The valley and hillsides have yielded about 10,000 historically significant items. An archaeological team has worked with the American Indians in recording the history of the region and there is talk of erecting an American Indian museum on MWD parkland. The strategy adopted by the water company of finding the least controversial site in the first place and then working with all interests from the beginning has ensured that a reservoir which will double the current amount of above-ground water storage in Southern California will begin construction in 1995 and near completion around the turn of the century with the minimal amount of conflict possible. Had this not happened, considering the scale of the project no one would have given the water company very good odds on securing the go-ahead.

Developing countries

Developing countries are now having to face what is for many the new challenge of public participation. For countries such as the Peoples Republic of China the EIA process is forcing the issue of public participation in decision making onto the public agenda. Many developing countries are highly dependent for their rapid development on foreign aid and grants from organisations such as the World Bank which are now insisting on the application of EIA as a condition of aid (see Chapter 12). Since public participation is a fundamental requisite of effective EIA such countries are faced with a real dilemma of opening up their decision making and political processes or receiving no aid. For many the choice of speeding up development has already been made so they are often faced with no alternative but to look seriously at public participation for the first time.

This is no easy task in China, for example, where the scale and pace of development is so enormous that the normal issues associated with Western development pale into insignificance. Take the example of the Three Gorges Dam project which would create a reservoir out of 600 kilometres (365 miles) of the Yangtze River to produce some 17,000 MW of hydro-electricity. The height of the dam would be 175 metres. This one project alone would displace some 1.2 million people from the surrounding land, submerging 100 towns and villages and 44,000 hectares of land. It seems unlikely that by Western standards a project of such scale and impact would be allowed to proceed. In the first place the people affected would need to participate in the EIA process or at least be consulted prior to a decision being made. Secondly, if the magnitude and significance of environmental impacts have any bearing on decision making there would seem to be a strong case in this instance for rejecting the proposal altogether. In China the public have not been consulted. Consequently, the feasibility study carried out by CIPM Yangtze Joint Venture (CYJV) and sponsored and endorsed by the Canadian International Development Agency (CIDA), has been much criticised (Probe International/Earthscan, 1993; Fearnside, 1993). In the face of such criticism the Canadians withdrew from further involvement. In India, the World Bank was forced to commission an independent review, and subsequently (in 1993) withdrew its funding of the Sardar Sarovar Dam project on the Namada River in Gujarat because the Indian Government had failed to involve the local Tadvi tribal people who were to be displaced, and had not addressed adequately the environmental impacts of the project.

The Chinese authorities are now having to struggle with the concept of public participation in a political regime where the public is not consulted, yet where the commercial imperative has now firmly taken hold and the country is increasingly being opened up to Western influences. The Chinese are now well down the road towards a less closed and a more 'market-based' system, led by rapid economic development, however uneasy the authorities may feel. The social upheaval which is set to follow is likely to be immense as may be the ultimate impact on the nature and scale of the intended development programmes if, or perhaps when, the public finally have a say.

How it ought to be

Figure 6.1 illustrates the opportunities that can exist for public participation throughout the EIA process, although under current legislation in the UK and many other systems the only formal requirement for public consultation occurs on publication of the (final) environmental impact statement.

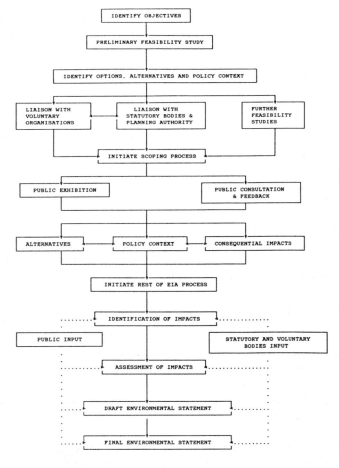

Figure 6.1 Opportunities for public participation in the EIA process (after Sheate, 1991)

Chapter 7

ENFORCEMENT

EIA is effective only when enforced. Interesting comparisons can be made between the enforcement mechanisms (or lack of such mechanisms) of various legal regimes.

Europe

The UK Government has failed to establish an effective form of quality control. Not only is there inadequate review of decisions over the requirement for EIAs in the UK there is no effective quality control over the information provided by the developer (the environmental statement or ES) to the competent authority. This is especially true where the competent authority is also the developer. This has led to poor quality ESs slipping through the system with no consistent check, review or feedback mechanism in place. Individual local authorities have often seen very few ESs to date and therefore do not always have the expertise to assess fully the adequacy of the information provided to them by a developer, although they have the power to request additional information. An 'ombudsman' agency able to hold up the decision-making process until the requirements of the EIA Directive had been met has been suggested as a solution to this problem (Cerny and Sheate, 1992; CPRE, 1992; Sheate and Cerny, 1993) and is explored further below.

A report commissioned by the UK Department of the Environment from the University of Manchester EIA Centre (UK DoE, 1991b) showed that out of a sample of 24 ESs examined, two thirds were judged to be unsatisfactory, failing to comply with the minimum requirements of Schedule 3 of the EIA Regulations. The report put forward a series of recommendations to improve the quality control of ESs. Further studies (eg Coles, Fuller and Slater, 1992; ENDS 1993) of more recent ESs suggest a gradual improvement in quality, although still some 30% or more of ESs can be considered inadequate.

Litigation in the UK is uncommon, largely because of the costs involved, both in supporting a case and if costs are awarded against the plaintiff should the case be lost. Third parties may also have difficulty in proving locus standi in the first place. There have been a handful of key cases in the UK since implementation of the EC Directive in 1988. These are dealt with in some detail in Chapter 9 where they particularly illustrate the relationship between EIA and conservation legislation and policy.

In the Netherlands, the EIA system is administered by the Commission for Environmental Impact Assessment (the Commission). Under the Environmental Protection (General Provisions) Act 1986 the duties of the Commission are to make recommendations on requests for exemptions from EIA requirements and to advise competent authorities on guidelines and contents of Environmental Impact Reports (EIRs). It is involved at both the scoping stage and review stage of each EIR. Recommendations made by the Commission must be taken into account by the decision-making authority. The Commission has, at times, chosen to become heavily involved in the technical aspects of individual cases, for example on Maastricht Airport where it employed its own consultants. Its recommendations, however, are not binding, nor does the Commission have powers to impose its will.

The Dutch EIA system places high value on certainty, ensuring that developers and government departments alike know when EIA is required.

In Flanders (Belgium) the project proponent takes the first step in the EIA process by deciding whether or not the project requires EIA. The proponent for any project needs to look to the detailed list of criteria found in the Flemish legislation which spells out exactly which types of project require EIA. The list is divided into two parts which correspond more or less to Annexes I and II of Directive 85/337/EEC. Each part of the list has been enacted in a separate decision or resolution of the Flemish Executive (the main legislation implementing the EC Directive being the Installations Decision - 'the Decision' - of 23 March 1989).

Once the proponent has concluded that EIA is required, it notifies the competent authority - the Environmental Department - of its intention to undertake the project. As part of its notice to the competent authority, the proponent must include, among other things, a list of the names and addresses of the experts who will make up the board responsible for assembling the EIS.

The Flemish legislation attempts to ensure that the EIS is assembled with the participation of objective experts by regulating the composition of the board and the qualifications of some of its members.

The proponent is responsible for assembling the board of experts according to the legally required standard. The law requires that at least one of the experts is chosen from among those listed by the government as 'approved' in up to nine speciality areas (for example: people, flora and fauna, sound and vibrations, monuments, landscapes and material goods generally). The idea is that the expert specialist will be charged with describing the effects likely to be caused in their specialist area so that the complete picture will emerge when all of the specialist reports are compiled.

In addition to the expert(s) chosen from the government list, the proponent must also appoint at least one expert who is not on the list to be responsible for "the technical and organizational measures to prevent a disturbance of the environment by the planned project". In practice this is most likely to be 'in-house' staff.

The procedural guidance that the board of experts receives comes from the Decision and from a written agreement reached with the proponent that is based upon it. The Decision requires that

> "if the board of experts has knowledge of reasonable alternative solutions, which would have less hazardous effects on the environment, then they should investigate and evaluate these".

It does not, however, require the investigation of any specific alternatives like the 'zero option' or the 'most environmentally friendly option'.

The proponent is required to ensure that the EIS is compiled in a manner compatible with law by concluding a written agreement with the board of experts. This agreement has to be based upon Chapter III of the Decision which specifies what the EIS must contain. Among other things, the agreement must require the board to include in the EIS a description of the

> "most likely alternative...investigated with a statement of the most prominent reason for their choice, in light of the environmental effects".

North America

In the US, while NEPA lacks an ombudsman agency charged with the enforcement of its requirements, the Council on Environmental Quality (CEQ) performs certain advisory functions. The CEQ is a small organization of modest resources which adopts regulations and supervises the adoption by individual agencies of procedures implementing NEPA. Due to its limited funds, however, the CEQ is largely prevented from participation in individual NEPA disputes.

The CEQ may, however, become involved in proposals of national importance, or through little used "referral" procedures under Part 1504 of the Regulations. Under the Clean Air Act 1963 (as amended) the Environmental Protection Agency may refer to the CEQ any proposed federal agency action which it determines is environmentally unsatisfactory. Moreover, under the Regulations, any federal agency may refer the proposed action of another agency to the CEQ if that action is of national importance and environmentally contentious. The CEQ then undertakes a review of the lead agency's compliance with NEPA procedures, during which no decision may be made on the proposal by the lead agency. While the CEQ may not ultimately prevent action on a proposal beyond 60 days, its findings may be used in subsequent litigation over the adequacy of NEPA compliance. Therefore, although the CEQ does not have ombudsman powers, the very existence of the referral procedures probably encourages agencies to follow NEPA requirements and to resolve disputes early.

In light of the CEQ's limited resources, and since NEPA's procedures are in large part effected by agencies internally, NEPA relies upon enforcement of its requirements by the courts. While NEPA litigation is widely viewed as costly and time consuming, it has successfully ingrained NEPA's requirements into the planning processes of federal agencies. In fact, while NEPA litigation constitutes the majority of environmental litigation against the United States Government, it is a negligible part of all the litigation against the Government.

The typical NEPA complaint is brought against a federal agency alleging that the requirements of NEPA were not followed in making the decision on a proposed action. Any citizen, or group of citizens, may file such a suit, as long as it is alleged that the citizen, or a member of the group, uses and enjoys the environmental resource threatened by agency action (Sierra Club v. Morton, 1972). The complaint may allege that an EIS or EIA should have been prepared or was inadequate. If the court agrees, it may halt the action until the procedural inadequacies are remedied. In this way, the courts concentrate not on the correctness of the agency's judgment, but on its compliance with procedure in making the judgment.

Like its federal counterpart, CEQA in California has not established an ombudsman agency to oversee the quality of EIRs. Similar to the CEQ, the Office of Planning and Research, including the State Clearinghouse, provides guidance and information but not supervision. Rather, the various lead agencies have the responsibility to ensure that EIRs under their jurisdictions meet CEQA requirements. CEQA has, like NEPA, relied upon the courts to enforce EIA standards.

Mechanisms of enforcement

There are two main ways in which enforcement can be achieved: litigation or through the establishment of an 'ombudsman' or enforcement agency. In the US the courts have been a crucial force in changing agency behaviour to include the environment in decision-making. In Canada, the Guidelines Order only assumed real significance when the courts held that it created judicially enforceable rights. In New Zealand the Ministry for the Environment oversees and is empowered to intervene in the EIA process. By contrast, in the UK and much of the EC the absence of either effective agencies or widespread litigation has proved to be one of the main stumbling blocks to improving the standard and extent of EIA. Enforcement becomes even more essential with SEA (see Part III), especially where a public agency is both a proponent and the judge in its own compliance with EIA requirements.

Both methods of enforcement, litigation and the ombudsman agency, have weaknesses. Private litigation involves daunting expense and delay, while often encouraging unwieldy EISs. More importantly, however, private litigation as an enforcement tool can only be effective in the presence of advanced judicial institutions combined with a tradition of use by the public. Such conditions exist in the US where litigation has generally been successful in enforcing EIA procedures. First, NEPA and CEQA emphasize procedural requirements, which can be interpreted and enforced by the courts. Second, the US public is generally familiar with the use of the courts for resolving disputes. Third, non-governmental organizations have concentrated their resources and political will on litigation to further their environmental causes. In many other countries inaccessibility to the courts, lack of litigious tradition, and high costs prevents litigation from assuming such significance.

Early on, the European Community decided that the litigious example of the United States would not be followed. Unfortunately, the EC has not yet established any alternative to litigation in Member States to ensure compliance with EIA requirements. It does, however, have a somewhat laborious complaints procedure under the Treaty of Rome for securing implementation of Directives.

The ombudsman agency, however, has its own problems. Often, the agency is not given sufficient powers or resources to ensure that EIA is properly done or, as in the Netherlands, its role is limited by, for example, applicability thresholds. There is also danger of wasteful inter-agency power struggles and a general reluctance on the part of Governments to intrude on the territory of established departments.

For litigation to be an effective enforcement tool it must already exist as part of the country's culture and provide wide public access to the courts as in the US. Unless such conditions prevail the only real alternative for securing compliance with EIA legislation is the establishment of a statutory enforcement body. Possible characteristics of such a body are many and varied.

In the Netherlands, for example, the EIA Commission has a clear advisory function, becoming involved in technical aspects of scoping and review of individual EIA proposals. On the other hand, its detailed involvement is made possible by the relatively small number of proposals passing the applicability threshold tests. It is not, however, able to prevent a decision being made even in cases of inadequate EIA compliance.

Under NEPA any agency can refer cases of inadequate EIA to the CEQ which can delay decision-making for up to 60 days during its review. This referral process is, however, purely persuasive, only available for proposals of national significance, and, in practice, is rarely used. Moreover, the CEQ is a small, advisory institution with limited resources.

In New Zealand under the Resource Management Act 1991 the Ministry for the Environment has the power to intervene in the EIA process, although this has so far been little used. New Zealand is, in fact, re-inventing many of the mistakes already experienced in the UK where day to day enforcement is left to inexperienced and inadequately resourced local authorities (Morgan, 1993 and pers.comm.). It is ironic that New Zealand has devolved responsibility to local authorities at the expense of an overseeing agency which maintains consistency and standards at the same time as practitioners in the UK are waking up to the need for just such an agency.

In Canada FEARO under the Guidelines Order performed merely advisory functions. While the CEAA may provide the Environment Minister with some new powers, its role in enforcement has yet to be seen.

The major pitfall of most of the agencies considered is their limitation largely to an advisory role. Given the intrinsically procedural nature of EIA, an enforcement agency's prime function should be to ensure that these procedures are met. An advisory agency, however, is severely limited in the extent to which it can do this. An illustration of the role of a proposed model EIA agency in enforcing compliance with procedures is shown in Figure 7.1 (Sheate and Cerny, 1993).

A crucial corollary of an enforcement agency having the power to hold up decision-making is that it is consulted by the proponent at the scoping stage so that the likelihood of delay later on is reduced. By way of example, possible legislative text for establishing such an agency in European Community Member States is suggested in Figure 7.2 (Sheate and Cerny, 1993). This model may, however, have much wider applicability.

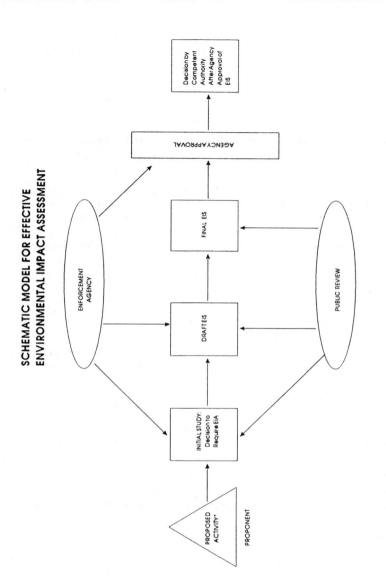

Figure 7.1 Schematic model for effective environmental impact assessment.

Figure 7.2 Suggested model enforcement structure for EIA in the European Community

Article (Scoping)

1. Member States shall take the measures necessary to ensure that, where it is appropriate, the lead authority or developer publishes a Draft Outline of the Report, which shall outline the proposed contents of the Report, prior to undertaking an environmental assessment of a proposed activity.

2. Pursuant to paragraph 1 above, the lead authority or developer shall submit the Draft Outline to the competent authority which shall make it available for public comment for a specified period and consult the Environmental Assessment Authority and other relevant bodies.

3. The Draft Outline shall contain a discussion of any environmental assessment report or reports already in existence from which the relevant Report will draw information, analysis, or mitigation measures.

Article (Draft and Final Report)

1. Member States shall take measures necessary to ensure that the developer or lead authority submits the Draft Report to the competent authority and shall consult other relevant bodies and the public on the basis of the Draft Report. The competent authority may request further information where necessary.

2. The developer or lead authority, after taking into account the views expressed pursuant to paragraph 1, shall submit the Final Report to the competent authority and make it available to the public. The competent authority shall consult the Environmental Assessment Authority on the compliance of the Final Report with the requirements of the Directive.

3. If the Environmental Assessment Authority is of the opinion that the requirements of this Directive have not been met it shall publish the reasons for this opinion, and consult with the developer or lead authority, and the competent authority, regarding the reasons for the failure to comply.

4. Pursuant to paragraph 3 above, the developer or lead authority and/or the competent authority may submit to the Environmental Assessment Authority the reasons for the Final Report's inadequacy, including technical difficulties, lack of know-how, and the previous inclusion of relevant components in an environmental assessment at another level in the decision-making process, which shall be taken into consideration by the Environmental Assessment Authority.

5. If, after taking into account this consultation, the Environmental Assessment Authority is of the opinion that the Final Report's inadequacy is unreasonable, it shall require that the decision by the competent authority regarding the proposed activity shall not be made until it is satisfied that the Final Report is brought into compliance with this Directive.

6. If the Environmental Assessment Authority considers the Final Report adequate, the competent authority shall take into account the Final Report, the opinion of relevant authorities and the comments of the public in reaching a decision about the proposed activity and its implementation.

The need for enforcement does not mean that the EIA system should be overly rigid. An unduly inflexible approach which constrains the application of EIA, for example through the use of high thresholds, is likely to impede its effectiveness and may thwart the evolution of procedures and techniques. Flexibility can best be promoted by the use of a broad application standard such as the significance test and SEA within a tiered system.

In addition, flexibility can be aided by placing primary responsibility for the preparation of the EIS with the proponent. This enables the content requirements of the EIS to be tailored to the specific circumstances of the proposal. It also encourages developers to incorporate EIA principles into their design and planning processes as a matter of course. One criticism often levied at EIA is that of developer bias in the preparation of the EIS; this is the main justification in Flanders for requiring authorised consultants to be used by developers, although in practice this does not appear to introduce real independence. Similarly, NEPA requires the authorizing federal agency to produce the EIS rather than the private developer. Developer bias should not, however, be a problem if an adequate enforcement framework exists. Not surprisingly, the absence of such an enforcement framework results all too often in the attempted mitigation of impacts rather than their avoidance.

The evidence available suggests a common reluctance by Governments to consider the establishment of adequate enforcement mechanisms or institutions with over-arching powers to enforce procedures across the territories of government departments. Yet, as can be seen, enforcement is critical to the success of EIA.

Chapter 8

POST-PROJECT MONITORING

Introduction

Post-project (or post-implementation) monitoring has tended to be the runt of the EIA litter of activities. More often than not it does not occur and when it does happen or is required it is as likely as not to be of poor quality and is frequently at the mercy of inadequate enforcement.

All in all, post-project monitoring does not have a very illustrious history, yet arguably it is one of the most important parts of the EIA process, especially if an EIA system is to mature effectively. Proposals for post-project monitoring should be included by a developer in an environmental statement and monitoring requirements may be required as conditions of planning permission by the planning authority. The crucial factor, however, is whether that post-project monitoring happens and what is done with that information. The iterative nature of EIA should be as much in evidence after the project has been built as it is during the design process.

Only by the knowledge, experience and understanding gathered as a result of post-project monitoring can the effectiveness of the earlier EIA processes, ie identification and assessment of impacts, be seen. Predictions made in an environmental statement need to be tested against the reality once that project has been built. That information should then inform best practice, government guidance and local authority attitudes to future EIAs, including the scope of issues that should be addressed, alternatives, mitigation measures, monitoring requirements and the effectiveness of particular methodologies.

EC Directive

The EC Directive on EIA is remarkably silent on the issue of post-project monitoring. The only reference that can be construed as being remotely connected with it is in Article 9 where it refers to the publication of

> "the content of the decision and any conditions attached thereto".

The European Commission's Five-Year review report (see Chapter 4) notes that most Member States, in line with the Directive, have not made their own additional provisions for post-project monitoring. The Commission found that monitoring was strongest where there were already strong requirements in existing procedures, but that monitoring procedures generally had not been improved in response to the Directive. The UK EIA regulations make no special provision for post-project monitoring although consent procedures, eg planning permission, may allow for conditions to be attached to the consent.

It is likely that the Commission will seek to introduce monitoring requirements into an amended Directive during 1994. Early unpublished drafts of proposed amendments have included provisions for amending Article 9 along the following lines:

> "Member States shall adopt the measures necessary to ensure that the effects arising from the implementation of the project will be monitored and that the results of the monitoring and the appropriate measures proposed by the competent authority to reduce or offset any significant adverse environmental effects revealed are made available to the public concerned and where appropriate to Member States likely to be significantly affected."

Espoo Convention on transboundary impacts

More encouraging than the EC Directive is the Espoo Convention on EIA in a transboundary context (Appendix 2) which makes specific provision for post-project monitoring and analysis. Article 7 of the Convention enables the Parties concerned, at the request of any of the Parties, to determine whether and how a post-project analysis should be carried out, specifically concerning the likely significant transboundary effects. Where a post-project analysis is undertaken it shall include the surveillance of the activity and the determination of any adverse transboundary impact. If the post-project analysis reveals significant adverse transboundary impacts the other Party must be informed and the concerned Parties must then consult on necessary measures to reduce or eliminate the impact.

Since the Espoo Convention makes provision for post-project analysis in a transboundary context, at the very least it would seem that the European Commission will have to amend the EC Directive to take this on board in order to ratify the Convention (Chapter 12), even if not for projects where there are no transboundary effects. If the requirement for post-project monitoring and analysis was drawn so as not to cover all projects this would surely stretch the subsidiarity argument to extremes. It is not difficult, however, given the current political climate, to see that card being played, leaving it up to Member States to determine whether and to what extent post-project monitoring or analysis is required for anything other than those projects likely to have transboundary effects. However, as the Commission has found, the effectiveness of EIA is influenced by the extent to which post-project monitoring takes place and it would seem entirely appropriate for the Directive to seek to ensure minimum standards of post-project monitoring. Some Member States such as the UK, Germany and Denmark have shown some hostility to any extension of the EIA Directive and might seek to block any or all amendments designed to improve the effectiveness of the Directive, especially where they might impose additional requirements and costs on developers or competent authorities.

The experience in the EC and Member States has clearly been that if post-project monitoring or analysis is not contained in legislation, it is unlikely to happen or be effective. There are occasions, especially for large schemes, where the developer may choose to carry out post-project monitoring and evaluation on a voluntary basis or where an authority may choose to carry out its own post-project 'audit'. Such an example can be seen in a post-project audit carried out by Manchester University EIA Centre on the Greater Manchester Metrolink scheme (Jones and Lee, 1993).

Where a tiered system of EIA and strategic environmental assessment (SEA) exists (see Chapter 10) each assessment at subsequent decision levels also acts as a form of post-decision monitoring. That is a further example of the iterative nature of EIA, not just within decision levels, but also between. At project level clearly there is no natural subsequent EIA process, as would be found at higher levels in a tiered system, and so post-project monitoring needs to be created to provide a similar opportunity for feedback. Post-decision monitoring at higher decision levels is just as important as post-project monitoring and also needs to be created in the absence of a tiered system, for example where policy appraisal (Chapters 10 and 11) might exist in isolation from project EIA: the UK Government's guidance on policy appraisal (UK DoE, 1991a) does include reference to the need to monitor and evaluate the policy to inform future decision making.

Australia

The importance of the post-project monitoring stage in the EIA process has been explicitly recognised in Australia where the role of EIA is now seen firmly in the context of 'ecologically' sustainable development (Sippe and Ashe, 1993; ANZECC, 1991) and included in the National Strategy for Ecologically Sustainable Development agreed in December 1992. Following a decision by First Ministers in 1990 to negotiate an Intergovernmental Agreement on the Environment, a national approach to EIA was developed through a working group set up by the Australian and New Zealand Environment and Conservation

Council (ANZECC). The Australian Intergovernmental Agreement on the Environment came into effect on 1 May 1992 and included a schedule on EIA based largely on the ANZECC 'National Approach'. That schedule sets out a comprehensive approach to EIA for Territory, State and the Commonwealth governments which includes a tiered approach to EIA and strategic environmental assessment, efforts to address cumulative impacts more effectively and a greater emphasis on post-implementation evaluation. Refreshingly, it also recognises that the EIA process is essentially judgemental rather than assuming that science based outcomes will provide all the answers.

Chapter 9

EIA AND CONSERVATION - DRAWING THE THREADS TOGETHER

Introduction

EIA has sometimes been seen by conservationists almost as some sort of panacea. The fact that it is preventative, seeking to avoid environmental damage before it happens, has tended to imbue EIA, at least in the minds of some people, with a greater degree of influence over decision making than it deserves. Once implemented, as we have seen in the UK, there can sometimes be a belief that legal action on the grounds of inadequate EIA or failure to require EIA will be an effective remedy and that the environmental damage will be prevented. Unfortunately this has not often proved to be the case.

Rightly, EIA has been seen as an important new weapon in the armoury available to conservationists. It brings the environment centre stage in decision making where previously it was not. It has the potential to encourage protection and conservation of environments, habitats and countryside otherwise unprotected by statutory designations. At the same time, because of the focus of EIA on the issue of significance, those areas that are protected by designations will tend to be better protected through EIA legislation, since action affecting those areas is, by definition, more likely to result in significant environmental effects and therefore be subject to EIA.

Conservationists, therefore, have also sought to use EIA legislation to reinforce existing conservation legislation, eg sites designated as Sites of Special Scientific Interest (SSSIs), Areas of Outstanding Natural Beauty (AONBs), Scheduled Ancient Monuments. The fact that EIA should provide information on the existing environment, as well as the likely significant effects a proposal may have on the environment, means that any other form of environmental protection legislation which applies to a particular area, or administrative, non-statutory forms of protection, should be identified through the EIA process and therefore taken into account in the decision making process. It also means that even where there are no designations, information on species and habitats, archaeological remains and historical landscapes should be made apparent in a systematic way: something that would not necessarily happen in the absence of a requirement for EIA.

The EC Directive specifies (Annex III) that EIA should include a description of aspects of the environment likely to be significantly affected by the proposed project, including, in particular, populations, fauna, flora, soil, water, air, climatic factors, material assets, including architectural and archaeological heritage, landscape and the inter-relationship between the above factors. Conservationists of all descriptions, whether they be wildlife, landscape, built environment or archaeological conservationists, can find benefits to be had from the EIA process. It means these issues must at least be considered: the first step on the way to such issues influencing the decision.

Whether these issues are considered and the extent to which they influence decisions is, of course, the stuff of litigation. Unfortunately, in the UK the amount of EIA case law is limited and gives little encouragement to anyone seeking legal remedies. The major barrier to litigation in the UK is cost, in particular the likelihood of the other side's costs being awarded against you should you lose the case. Consequently, few ordinary citizens and very few voluntary organisations are willing to risk legal bills of tens or hundreds of thousands of pounds. One of the consequences of this is that many people are resorting to a very cheap, but very cumbersome and unpredictable alternative: that of complaining to the European Commission about infringement of the EIA Directive (see below).

This chapter considers the implications of some of the most important UK EIA cases that have been brought so far.

Litigation has tended to seek judicial resolution for a number of key issues, most notably concerning so-called 'pipeline' cases - whether the EIA Directive applied to projects part way through the decision making process when the Directive came into effect; whether the Directive has direct effect, irrespective of the Member State implementing legislation; the poor quality and poor application of EIA including the failure to require EIA at all; and whether individuals or organisations have standing to bring legal action over EIA requirements. These issues are addressed in turn below.

'Pipeline' cases

The EC Directive makes no special transitional arrangements for projects part way through the decision making process. The Directive requires that projects should be subject to an assessment before consent is given (Article 2(1)). The interpretation by the European Commission has been that unless a project had been given consent before the date on which the Directive became effective an assessment would be required for an Annex I project and may have been required for an Annex II project. The Directive was due to come into effect on 3 July 1988.

In Twyford Parish Council v Secretary of State for the Environment and Secretary of State for Transport (the Twyford Down case) the issue at stake was whether and how the Directive applied to 'pipeline' projects, in this case a proposed section of motorway (M3) near Winchester in Hampshire. This was not simply a case of whether the Directive applied to the date of application for consent or the date of consent itself, since the implementing regulations (the Highways (Assessment of Environmental Effects) Regulations 1988 SI No 1241) include a provision exempting projects whose draft orders had been published before the date of 21 July 1988 (when the Regulations were published) from the requirements of the EIA Regulations. The fact that the implementing regulations exempted 'pipeline' projects raised the question of whether this was correct implementation of the Directive and if not whether the Directive had direct effect (see below). The fact that the Regulations were published on the 21 July, after the 3 July date for formal implementation, was not an issue in this case. The Twyford Down scheme had been in preparation for some considerable time. It had been formally proposed by the Secretary of State for Transport in 1987 and the formal public inquiry had been completed before July 1988. However, the Inspector's report of that inquiry was not published until October 1988 and the decision of the Secretaries of States to confirm the orders was not made until some twenty months after the Directive had come into force.

McCullogh J held that 'environmental assessment' as envisaged by the EC Directive is not simply an environmental study but that it is a process of some considerable duration and that it is to influence that process at every stage:

> "To treat the environmental considerations in isolation or to begin to take them into account at any stage later than the earliest would run counter to the clear intention of the ` Directive."

He concluded that the absence of transitional arrangements from the Directive was significant. Had it been the intention of the Directive to apply to pipeline cases one could have expected the Directive to make appropriate provision. This view, of course, runs counter to that of the European Commission.

The difficulty presented by pipeline cases is clear. If, as McCullogh J held, the Directive does not apply to pipeline cases it is possible to envisage two extreme cases. The first is where a project has completed virtually all its stages of the consent procedure, except final consent before the date of implementation. The second is where an application for consent has been made just before the date of implementation, but where the project has not yet embarked on the various stages of the consent procedure. In the first case, it would appear to be highly retrospective to apply the Directive and therefore McCullogh J's interpretation would appear to be correct, but equally the second may have escaped the requirements of EIA by a whisker.

Macrory (1992a) argues that the Directive does expressly provide a mechanism for dealing with cases where decision making had almost been completed before July 1988 and which would avoid the practical consequences of retrospectively imposing a lengthy set of new procedures. Article 2 (3) of the Directive allows Member States to exempt "in exceptional cases" a specific project in whole or in part from the provisions laid down in the Directive. Where a Member State chooses to do so they must consider whether another form of assessment would be "appropriate" and make information relating to the exemption available to the public, and inform the Commission, prior to granting consent, of the reasons justifying the exemption. The Directive does not define an 'exceptional' case, but a case where much of the decision making process had already been completed would appear to be an appropriate reason for exemption under Article 2 (3). It is unclear why the UK Government did not utilise Article 2 (3) to exempt the Twyford Down case explicitly from the requirements of the EIA Directive, unless it believed that the exemption of schemes for which draft orders had been published prior to July 1988 in the implementing Highways Regulations, which had been notified to the European Commission, was sufficient.

In another road scheme case, that of Lewin and Rowley v Secretary of State for the Environment and Secretary of State for Transport (1989), the appellants objected to the draft order for the A1-M1 link road which would cross the historic field of the Battle of Naseby. A public inquiry into the draft orders had been held between 1984-85 with the inspector's report being published in July 1986. The Secretaries of State's decision letter was given on 6 April 1987 and the definitive order was made on 10 December 1987 to come into force on 5 February 1988. Clearly, all the steps in the decision making process had been completed before July 1988.

The appellants argued, perhaps somewhat obtusely, that the Highways Regulations were founded on a misinterpretation of the Directive. They argued that 'development consent' could not properly be given until the statutory appeal against the order had been determined or until contracts had been placed for carrying out the proposed works. The appellants requested the

Court either to enforce the Directive (by direct effect) or make reference to the European Court of Justice as to when 'development consent' is given. Dillon LJ held that English Law as set out in the Highways Regulations complied with the requirements of the Directive and that no EIA was needed because "the draft order and, indeed, the definitive order were both made well before the statutory instrument came into effect". He declined to refer the matter to the European Court because the definitive order had been made before the Directive came into force.

The definitive order, as the Court of Appeal held, would appear to be a "consent which entitles the developer to proceed with the project" according to Article 1(2) of the Directive. This is the final consent from a 'competent authority' before a developer can proceed; a court of law is not, after all, a competent authority as far as authorisation for road building is concerned. The argument that consent is not given until contracts are let had little merit since the consent procedures to which the Directive relates are those of the Highways Act 1980 and not the procedures relating to the letting of public contracts.

Direct effect of the EIA Directive

The issue of direct effect of the EIA Directive arose in the Twyford Down case (above). McCullogh J consider what would have been the implications had he held that the Directive did apply to projects which had started on the decision making process prior to July 1988. He concluded that the applicants were among those whom the Directive was intended to benefit and that its provisions were unconditional and sufficiently precise to have direct effect according to the European Court (Becker v Finanzamt Munster-Innenstadt (1982)). The road scheme in question was, of course, an Annex I project although the judgement did not address this fact.

Mr Justice McCullogh went on to answer the question whether, in addition, the applicants had to demonstrate that they had suffered in consequence of the failure to implement the Directive correctly. He concluded that the Directive could not be enforced by someone who had not suffered. He went on to consider that if the Directive applied, were its terms breached? The applicants argued that a 'non-technical summary' had not been prepared, as required under Article 5(2). He considered that the burden must lie with the applicants to show failure and, as counsel for the Secretaries of State argued, this must involve demonstrating that what was provided could not reasonably have been regarded by anyone in the position of Secretary of State as sufficient for the purpose (Wednesbury unreasonableness). The Secretaries of State's counsel, with which Mr Justice McCullogh agreed, argued that the Inspector's report of the 1985 public inquiry could reasonably be regarded as being a non-technical summary. It is hard to see how anyone with even a scant knowledge of inspectors' reports (often running to hundreds of pages) and environmental statements, let alone EIA best practice, could reasonably consider an inspector's report to be a non-technical summary! A case, perhaps, of the judiciary being environmentally myopic? (Woolf, 1992).

Another important case which addressed the issue of direct effect is that of the Petition of Kincardine and Deeside District Council (Court of Session, 8 March 1991), known as the Glendye case. This was also the first decision of the Scottish higher courts dealing with EC environmental law. In this case the District Council challenged a decision of the Forestry Commissioners to approve an application for a grant for afforestation of a moorland without considering whether an EIA was required. There is no formal consent procedure in the UK for afforestation projects (see Chapter 5). The EC Directive has been implemented, albeit only partially, with respect to forestry projects through the grant aid procedure. The Environmental Assessment (Afforestation) Regulations 1988 came into force on 15 July 1988. In this case an application was made by Gladstone (1987) Settlements ('Fasque Estates') under the Woodland Grant Scheme on 8 July 1988, registered by the Forestry Commission on 13 July 1988. The area of new tree planting at Glendye was in excess of 1000 ha. Following discussion between the applicant and the Forestry Commission a revised application was submitted in October 1988 relating to 887 ha. The application was finally approved on 9 November 1990. Lord Coulsfield concluded that the application was made on 13 July and therefore the Regulations did not apply. However, since the Directive was due to come into force on 3 July 1988 the court went on to consider whether the EIA Directive had direct effect in this case. Lord Coulsfield held that the Forestry Commissioners could be regarded as a manifestation of the state. He also concluded that had the project fallen in Annex I and therefore under Article 4(1) that there would be a powerful argument that it should have direct effect since there are basic requirements which are sufficiently precise and unconditional. However, he felt unable to read Article 4(2) as being precise and unconditional because of the discretion given to Member States in the way in which Annex II projects which are to be subject to EIA are determined. In Lord Coulsfield's view, even if no regulations had been made in relation to forestry there would have been no breach:

> "The discretion conferred by Article 4(2) is not a discretion as to the means of implementation but a discretion as to whether steps should be taken at all in the particular context."

This conclusion of the court flies in the face of the view of the European Commission, accepted by the UK Government which was forced to accept that it was obliged to implement EIA requirements for Annex II and did not have the discretion to do nothing. One lawyer for the Commission (Williams, 1991) has argued that the discretion conferred by Article 4(2) should be read in conjunction with Article 2 which requires that projects likely to have significant effects are made subject to assessment procedures (see also Chapter 3).

> "...the Directive does, therefore, have direct effect where an Annex II project will have significant effects on the environment such that no Member State could reasonably have exercised its Article 4(2) discretion and decided otherwise."

(Williams, 1991)

Macrory (1992a) expresses some doubt as to the practicalities of using the direct effect doctrine for regulating the way the

Directive is applied in Member States as far as Annex II projects are concerned. For one thing, the history of the development of the Directive indicates that common criteria and guidelines for Member States to apply in determining which Annex II projects should be subject to EIA were proposed but never accepted (Sheate and Macrory, 1989). The delegation of that task to Member States has inevitably introduced a large measure of discretion (and discrepancy) and therefore practical difficulty in applying the direct effect doctrine to Annex II projects.

That the Directive has direct effect for Annex I projects would not appear to be in dispute and the decisions of both the Twyford Down and the Glendye case support this. Dr Ludwig Kramer of the European Commission also suggests that the Directive has direct effect with respect to Annex I projects (Kramer, 1991).

In an Irish case, that of Michael Brown v An Bord Pleanala (High Court of Eire, 27 July 1989), the issue of direct effect arose with respect to whether An Bord Pleanala (the Irish administrative body which decides planning appeals) was an organ of the state to which the doctrine applied. The plaintiffs had claimed that an environmental impact study submitted by Merrell Dow with their planning application for a pharmaceutical plant in the County of Cork did not comply with the Directive because it did not address the direct and indirect effects of possible pollution from the plant on cattle and tourism. An Bord Pleanala and Cork County Council both accepted that the Directive was applicable and that it had been complied with. Merrell Dow, while claiming that their EIA had met the terms of domestic legal requirements and of the Directive argued that the Directive could not be binding on them because a mere circular letter was insufficient to incorporate it properly into Irish domestic law. Barron J accepted Merrell Dow's arguments and concluded that:

> "Unless the principles of the Directive are already incorporated in the domestic law in the Member State, they do not have the force of law in the Member State unless they have been made legally binding by a domestic legislative process."

First, this conclusion assumes that EC Directives must be implemented only through legislation. The Treaty of Rome requires only that the aims of the Directive are achieved by introducing and using whatever legal or administrative machinery is necessary to do so. However, the European Court has elaborated on this over the years in finding that Directives should be implemented in a sufficiently robust and formal way. Second, and more importantly, it ignores entirely the possibility of the doctrine of direct effect being applicable. On the question as to whether An Bord Pleanala was an organ of the state Mr Justice Barron held that it was not because it could

> "in no way be held responsible for the failure of the State to implement the Directive, if failed they have."

This decision has been widely criticised in Irish legal circles (Scannell, 1990), since in other Irish cases, an Area Health Authority, a Chief Constable and the Irish Minister of Social Welfare have all been found to be bound by the direct effect principle.

This decision also conflicts with Costanzo v Commune di Milano (June 1989) which held that public bodies such as local authorities are obliged under Community law to ensure the application of directly effective provisions of Directives in all their decision making and related activities. In practice this may have to be raised during administrative proceedings such as public inquiries to ensure that the relevant authority is fully aware of its legal obligations (Macrory, 1992b).

Poor application of the Directive

The issue of poor application of the EIA Directive has been the focus for a large number of formal complaints to the European Commission (see below). However, it has also arisen in a number of cases of litigation. Poor application relates to the fact that while the appropriate legal and administrative machinery might be in place, in practice there is still a failure to implement the Directive.

One such case was that of R v Poole Borough Council ex parte Bee Bee and others (December 1990), also known as the Canford Heath case. The local authority, Poole Borough Council had proposed a local housing development on a heathland Site of Special Scientific Interest (SSSI) (Canford Heath) in Dorset. Since it was the authority's own proposal it was also the consenting (competent) authority. The authority granted itself planning permission, even though there were objections from the Nature Conservancy Council (the statutory conservation agency) and the World Wide Fund for Nature (UK). The case was taken to judicial review by WWF (UK) and the British Herpetological Society on the grounds that the local authority had not taken into consideration the fact that the site was an SSSI and that the authority had failed to consider whether an EIA should be carried out.

It transpired that the local authority had not considered whether the proposed project would fall under the Town and Country Planning EIA Regulations, let alone whether it would be likely to have a significant effect on the environment. Had this been considered the project might have been deemed to be an 'urban development project' under Schedule 2 (10)(b) of the regulations. Schiemann J held that the weight to be given to the fact that the site was an SSSI was solely for the authority. If special weighting was to be given to such a designation it required the Government to either legislate or to publish policy guidance to that effect.

Mr Justice Schiemann acknowledged that the local authority had not addressed the EIA regulations or the likelihood of significant effects, but that since it had had the objections of the environmental bodies before it he considered that the local authority had all the necessary information upon which to base a judgement. Schiemann J held that it was quite within the local authority's discretion to take such a decision, and that the authority had struck a lawful balance between the demands of conservation and the need for more housing. He therefore refused to quash the planning permission. This decision ignores the important procedural differences introduced by EIA, including the importance of public participation and the formal consideration of specific environmental information.

Arguably, it also violates the principle of European Law that domestic law cannot be relied upon contrary to a directive (Alder, 1993). The European Court in Marleasing v La Commercial Internacional de Alimentacion (November 1990) has held that national courts have a broad duty to interpret all national laws in the light of Community law or in such a way as not to frustrate the purpose of Community law which must predominate. The principle appears to apply whether the national law was passed before or after the relevant Community legislation, or whether or not it was passed in order to implement the Community law.

In March 1991, the Secretary of State for the Environment, Mr Michael Heseltine, revoked planning permission for the housing development because of the implications for this important national and international conservation site.

In R v Swale Borough Council and the Medway Ports Authority ex parte the Royal Society for the Protection of Birds (1990) the RSPB challenged the granting of planning permission by Swale Borough Council to the Medway Ports Authority for land reclamation of mudflats important for wintering birds (Lappel Bank), which was part of a larger scheme involving the construction of a storage area for cargo and a marina, on the grounds that it was a breach of both the EIA Directive and the EC Birds Directive. In the English Town and Country Planning EIA Regulations paragraph 1 (f) of Schedule 2 refers to "the reclamation of land from the sea". Paragraph 1 concerns activities for the purposes of agriculture. The applicants argued that paragraph 1 (f) of Schedule 2 should be interpreted so as to include land reclaimed for other purposes and that this would bring the English Regulations into line with the Directive and require the local authority to consider whether EIA was required. It is difficult to see how the applicants could have argued this since the Directive does not imply that 'reclamation of land from the sea' relates to anything other than agricultural activities: it is included in Annex II, paragraph 1 (h). If it was intended to apply more widely why was it not included in the miscellaneous category, Annex II paragraph 11: 'Other projects' rather than the 'Agriculture' category?

However, the Directive, under Annex II, paragraph 1 (d) does include, attached to the category of afforestation, 'land reclamation for the purposes of conversion to another type of land use'. But, even this category occurs under the overall category of 'Agriculture' represented by paragraph 1, which only adds to the confusion. It might also be construed that as this category is defined as distinct from 'reclamation of land from the sea' (para. 1 (h)) that any land reclaimed according to para. 1 (d) might refer to terrestrial land, as opposed to that reclaimed from the sea. These categories could usefully be clarified by amendments to the Directive.

The construction of a storage area for cargo and a marina, however, might be considered to fall with Annex I (trading ports) or Annex II (harbours etc not in Annex I). Simon Brown J held that the question must be answered strictly in relation to the development applied for, not any development contemplated beyond that. This conclusion allowed what was in effect a larger project to be broken up into smaller parts, thereby escaping the EIA regulations.

In addition, Simon Brown J held that the question of whether an EIA is required or whether a project falls within Schedule 1 or 2 of the EIA regulations was exclusively for the planning authority to decide subject only to traditional Wednesbury challenge (unreasonableness). In relation to whether the regulations correctly implemented the Directive, Mr Justice Simon Brown concluded that to adopt the interpretation suggested by the applicants would require "torturing the construction of these regulations beyond breaking point". Although the Marleasing decision had not yet been decided by the European Court of Justice regarding the doctrine of sympathetic interpretation (the duty to interpret national law in conformity with Community law), the principle that national legislation which is intended to implement Community measures must be interpreted in conformity with the parent Community legislation had been established in the case of von Colson and Kamman v Land Nordrhein Westfalen (1984). This principle had also been accepted and applied in the English courts on a number of occasions prior to the domestic EIA cases (Ward, 1993).

One of the most recent EIA cases to come before the courts is that of R v Secretary of State for Transport ex parte Surrey County Council (1993) in relation to proposals by the Department of Transport to widen and add three-lane link roads alongside the M25 motorway in Surrey which would result in a highway of 14 lanes in total. Surrey County Council applied to the High Court to seek permission to bring the decision of the Secretary of State to propose the roads before judicial review on the grounds that under the EIA Directive the proposed 'improvements' to the M25 between junctions 10 and 21 should be treated as one project, not as several separate schemes as intended by the Department of Transport. Their application for judicial review was refused on the grounds that the application was premature, since there was as yet no environmental statement. However, MacPhearson J accepted their argument, adding that he would expect the environmental statement when published to take into account all the Department's plans for the M25. Should the Department fail to incorporate such plans into the assessment Mr Justice MacPhearson stated that Surrey County Council would then be in a position to reapply to the court. In his decision the judge said that a new motorway over green fields could not be split up into individual schemes for the purposes of EIA, whereas an improvement of an existing motorway could be so split up. Surrey County Council have argued that it is stretching the imagination to call the proposals for the M25 simply an improvement.

Standing

One crucial question which has arisen in many of the cases discussed so far is that of who has locus standi (standing) to bring an action before the courts on the grounds of breach of EIA requirements.

In the Canford Heath case (R v Poole BC), Schiemann J found that WWF (UK) could only be considered as having 'sufficient interest' because they had made grants since 1971 to the British Herpetological Society (BHS) to assist in their work on habitats for sand lizards and smooth snakes, and had made their application jointly with BHS. The fact that WWF (UK) had been involved in the conservation of Dorset heathlands for over fifteen years and was an accredited participant at meetings of the contracting parties to the Bern Convention since 1986 would not, in the judge's view, have given them sufficient interest alone.

In the Glendye case (Petition of Kincardine and Deeside DC) Lord Coulsfield held that the petitioners could properly be said to have a reasonable concern with a major project in their area which may affect the economy or amenity of the area generally. They therefore had a material or sufficient interest. Lord Coulsfield had specifically rejected a rights-based test of standing for the EIA Directive (Macrory, 1992a), in contrast to the decision of McCullogh J in the Twyford Down case.

In the Twyford Down case, Mr Justice McCullogh took the view that the decisions of the European Court on direct effect implied that an individual must have 'suffered' in some way as a result of failure to implement the Directive in order to raise the question of direct effect. As they had not suffered in such a way they could not rely on the Directive, even though he held the relevant provision of the Directive had direct effect and that the applicants were amongst those whom the Directive was intended to benefit. Geddes (1992) suggests that McCullogh J relied too heavily on the case of Becker v Finanzamt Munster - Innenstaat (1982) which held that only an applicant who has "suffered as a consequence of the state's failure to implement the Directive in question" could rely on its provisions. Geddes points out that Becker was not concerned with locus standi which is a matter for national law dependent upon whether the applicants had sufficient interest. Macrory (1992a) points out that different Member States are already applying different rules of standing to the EIA Directive and that this issue needs to be addressed more directly at European level, either by the European Court or through Community legislation.

In the case of Swale (R v Swale BC) the RSPB was recognised as having sufficient interest to bring a case since the Council had promised and failed to consult on the proposed reclamation of the mud flats. In deciding not to grant relief to the RSPB,

Simon Brown J exercised a statutory discretion under the Supreme Court Act 1981 which allows the High Court to refuse leave if there "has been undue delay in making the application" and if the court considers that "the granting of the relief sought would be likely to cause substantial hardship to, or substantially prejudice the rights of, any person or would be detrimental to good administration." The application by the RSPB had been made two days before the expiry of a three-month statutory time limit. The Court decided that the developers interests would be prejudiced by quashing the planning permission since the work had already started and decided against granting relief to the RSPB.

However, subsequent to the Swale decision, the European Court of Justice has held in Emmott v Minister for Social Welfare (1991) that national authorities cannot rely on domestic limitation periods to frustrate a directly effective measure which has not been properly transposed into national law. Time cannot begin to run until proper transposition has been achieved (Ward, 1993). It would therefore appear that an applicant's delay is irrelevant if directly enforceable rights arise under the EIA Directive which have not been introduced into domestic law.

Ward (1993) suggests that should the issue of delay arise again in relation to the EIA Directive the court should first ascertain the goals of the Directive, then determine whether it has direct effect (including whether the applicants are the intended beneficiaries of the rights claimed) and then decide if these goals can be guaranteed by the relevant domestic regulations. If the answer to this last point is 'no' then Article 5 of the Treaty of Rome obliges the national judge to set aside domestic measures if they block directly effective rights (as held in R v Secretary of State for Transport ex parte Factortame Ltd, 1991). In practice, a fundamental question such as this should not really be answered for the first time by a national court without reference to the European Court of Justice.

The question of standing in UK courts, and the often narrow interpretation of who has standing, is a crucial one and, along with the issue of costs, severely limits the amount of litigation pursued by members of the public or voluntary, non-governmental organisations.

Sir Harry Woolf (Lord Justice of Appeal) in giving the 5th Garner Environmental Law Lecture in 1991 referred to the approach to locus standi taken in the case of R v Secretary of State for the Environment, ex parte Rose Theatre Trust (1989). The case, although nothing to do with EIA, concerned the remains of an Elizabethan theatre in London on a site awaiting redevelopment. The Secretary of State had refused to designate the remains as a listed building and the applicants attempted to challenge the Secretary of State's decision by application for judicial review. The applicants were concerned about locus standi and formed themselves into a trust company aimed at preserving the remains of the theatre. Schiemann J concluded that the decision not to designate the remains was

> "one of those governmental decisions in respect of which the ordinary citizen does not have a sufficient interest to entitle him to obtain leave for judicial review".

The judge held that since an individual would not have standing so

> "an aggregate of individuals could not claim sufficient interest not possessed by any of its members".

The trust therefore had no locus standi to bring the application. The problem, as Lord Justice Woolf pointed out, is that if the trust did not have locus standi who would? Had the decision of the Secretary of State been unlawful (which it was not), according to the decision of Schiemann J no one would appear to have been able to challenge it. A consistent, and liberal view of locus standi is needed urgently either from a higher national court, from the European Court of Justice or through Community legislation.

Complaints to the European Commission

The easy, cheap, although not necessarily any more effective, alternative to EIA litigation in the UK is to make a formal complaint to the European Commission which is charged with ensuring the enforcement of Community legislation Two examples are addressed in some detail in Chapter 10. A number of the cases addressed above have also been pursued through complaints to the European Commission although action relating to Twyford Down, for example, was eventually dropped.

In October 1991 the European Commission sent a detailed and lengthy Letter of Formal Notice, under Article 169 of the Treaty of Rome, to the UK Government describing various infringements of the EIA Directive, including individual cases and alleged failure to fully implement the Directive. The Commission alleged that the UK was in breach of the Directive in four general respects: first, the issue of pipeline cases (addressed above); second, the failure to require EIA for certain types of activities, notably agriculture, forestry and Crown development; third, that the UK is applying too broad a discretion in deciding which projects should be subject to EIA, and that the test of significance is an objective test; finally, that an assessment must be recorded in writing by the competent authority. More detail on a number of these points relating to implementation can be found in Chapter 5.

The Article 169 letter referred to above also included seven specific projects for which it alleged EIA had not been carried out properly. These included the M3 at Twyford Down, the East London River Crossing at Oxleas Wood, a proposed Coca-Cola plant in Northamptonshire, a BP oil refinery in Scotland, and the Channel Tunnel Rail Link. All of these were subsequently withdrawn, either because the projects themselves were withdrawn or because the requirements of the Directive were met to the satisfaction of the Commission. Infringement proceedings are inevitably highly political and the action described above resulted in considerable public and political controversy, not least because of the coincidence with debates over the Maastricht Treaty on European Union. Such infringement action will tend to be resolved wherever possible through mutual agreement, rather than it being taken finally by the European Commission to the European Court. There have been suggestions that the specific allegations relating to individual projects, such as Twyford Down and the Channel Tunnel Rail Link, were dropped in return for the UK Government agreeing to amend the implementing regulations in line with the view of the Commission.

The complaint procedure is an unsatisfactory mechanism for enforcing the spirit, even if not the requirements, of the EIA Directive. First, it provides an ineffective remedy for individual cases, especially where poor application is concerned or where there is poor quality of an environmental statement. The complaint procedure is intended to resolve primarily issues of principle to do with implementation of Community law, not to provide relief to complainants over individual projects. Therefore, because the EIA Directive is procedural, the Commission can only take action so long as there is a failure to comply with the procedures laid down in the Directive. If the Member State subsequently complies with the requirements of the Directive the Commission no longer has grounds for action. Again, this is particularly apposite with respect to individual cases, eg a failure to provide a non-technical summary is very easily resolved. The second problem with the complaint procedure is that the Commission is not obliged to pursue infringement action even if there is a breach of Community law (see the Wilton case in Chapter 10), and that it is unlikely to be open to an individual to seek any legal remedy against the Commission for failure to do so (Lord Bethell v Commission, 1982). Finally, the procedure is very slow and laborious and generally inappropriate if urgency is of the essence.

The fact that the complaint procedure is being pursued in so many cases is an indication of the failure of Member States and the Directive to establish effective national enforcement mechanisms and the general inaccessibility of the litigation process to the public (see Chapter 7).

Part III

TREADING A NEW PATH: STRATEGIC ENVIRONMENTAL ASSESSMENT

Chapter 10

THE TIERED APPROACH

Introduction

Defining the parameters of a project inevitably results in difficulties in deciding what constitutes a project as opposed to a programme or plan. A project may comprise a number of smaller sub-projects and a programme may comprise a series of projects. A plan may identify future projects or programmes or it may be a 'masterplan' covering a number of projects which are to be built or developed simultaneously or separately over a period of time. The fact that it is difficult to define precisely where the boundaries between these definitions should lie is itself an illustration of the value of a tiered approach to EIA which ensures that impacts on the environment are assessed at all the appropriate opportunities and at the degree of detail appropriate to the level of decision making.

Until recently, EIA has been applied largely to project level decision making, ie decisions about whether to go ahead with individual discrete development projects. In most cases it is not too difficult to recognise an individual project proposal, eg a factory, an oil terminal, an airport runway, a reservoir proposal, a housing development. However, there are cases where a development proposal comprises several discrete sub-projects. In the absence of any level of strategic environmental assessment (SEA) it is appropriate and arguably legitimate to say that the overall proposal is a 'project' made up of associated, ancillary or subsidiary projects.

Where a tiered system of SEA is established, however, this semantic distinction is rendered unnecessary since such a proposal would be caught at the programme level. This difficulty is clearly seen in two examples from the UK (discussed in detail below) which illustrate both the potential to draw the legal definition of 'project' under the EC Directive as widely as possible and the limitations of the same Directive in applying so far only to projects.

Case Study 1:Wilton Power Station, Teesside

In April 1991 a complaint was made to the then Environment Commissioner, Sr Carlo Ripa di Meana, of the European Commission in Brussels against the UK Secretary of State for Energy concerning the EIA carried out for the 1725 MW gas-fired combined heat and power (CHP) station at Wilton, Teesside, proposed by Teesside Power Limited (TPL) (a consortium including Enron Corporation, ICI and four regional electricity companies) (CPRE, 1991c; Sheate, 1992b). Consent had been given for this station in November 1990 without, it was argued, the full environmental effects of the proposal having been properly considered.

The power station falls under Annex I of the EC Directive on Environmental Impact Assessment (85/337/EEC) and therefore required a mandatory EIA. However, the overall project involved, in addition to the building of the power station, four other components:-

- a new natural gas pipeline

- a gas reception and processing facility

- a CHP fuel pipeline from the processing facility to the CHP facility

- new overhead power transmission lines and system upgrades (some 90 km of 400 kV lines).

131

It was this latter component of the power station project which gave rise to most concern.

Consent for the power station was given by the Secretary of State for Energy on 5 November 1990, on the basis of the information provided in the environmental statement for the project. The environmental statement did not include a description or assessment of the effects of the associated power transmission lines, the gas pipeline, the processing facility or the CHP fuel pipeline. While separate environmental impact assessments are required for these developments, the complaint argued that, under the EC Directive, the main environmental effects of the associated developments should have been considered under the EIA for the power station.

Concern was expressed that the Secretary of State did not see fit to require further information on these aspects, as he is entitled to do under the UK's own implementing legislation [Regulation 10 of The Electricity and Pipe-line Works (Assessment of Environmental Effects) Regulations 1990, SI no. 442]. Teesside Power Limited had successfully received consent for the power station even though the major impacts on the environment of the electricity transmission lines, the gas pipeline, the gas processing facility and the CHP pipeline did not feature in the accompanying documentation provided to the Secretary of State for Energy. Since the relevant information was not available to the Secretary of State - nor did he request such information - it was argued that his decision may not have been the same had all the relevant information been available to him.

The EC Directive on Environmental Impact Assessment (85/337/EEC) requires, under article 3 and Annex III, an environmental impact assessment to identify, describe and assess, where appropriate, the direct, indirect and secondary effects of a project on the environment. This information is required, where it is appropriate and relevant to the proposed project, to be provided to the competent authority - in this case the Secretary of State for Energy - before a decision on consent is taken. The environmental statement for the power station makes it clear that separate consent and environmental impact assessment procedures would be followed, by other companies, for the other aspects of the project, ie the transmission lines, the pipelines and the processing facilities. This piecemeal approach militates against a proper assessment of the environmental impact of the development of the power station and, it was argued, clearly contravenes the Directive's requirements that all direct, indirect and secondary effects of a project should be addressed, where appropriate.

The complaint suggested that it was not sufficient to argue that such information need not be included because it is dealt with by separate consent procedures or it is not relevant to a given consent procedure (article 5 (1)(a) of the Directive). Article 5 (1)(a) also refers to the relevance of the information

> "...to the specific characteristics of a particular project or type of project and of the environmental features likely to be affected",

and that this, together with the requirements of article 3 and Annex III suggests that such information would be highly relevant to the consent procedure for the power station itself.

The environmental effects of the transmission lines and other consequential developments associated with the power station should have been addressed as part of the EIA for the power station itself. Not to do so devalues the EIA of the main project and the effectiveness of the EIA Directive itself. The question was: should the Secretary of State for Energy have required further information, including information of the likely significant effects on the environment of the associated development of transmission lines, pipe-lines and processing facilities, before taking a decision and granting consent for the power station?

As indicated by the environmental statement for the power station, the procedures established after privatisation by the Electricity Act 1989 have separated the consent and environmental impact assessment procedures for power stations and transmission lines. The National Grid Company now has an obligation to connect a new electricity generator into the national grid, and is required to carry out its own EIA for new lines and major system upgrades. As seen in this case, this happens after the power station has been given consent, and any assessment of the environmental impact of the power lines carried out by NGC can have no influence on the decision over whether the power station should have been built in the first place. Yet the environmental impact of a power station is far more than simply its land-take, for example. Prior to the Electricity Act 1989 the then Central Electricity Generating Board (CEGB) considered the need for transmission lines as part of its application and consent procedures for a new power station. Indeed, the CEGB (1988), in their evidence to the Hinkley C public inquiry, argued that the siting of a new power station in the south, rather than the north, of the country was their preferred option partly because of reduced reliance on transmission of power over long distances and lower transmission losses. The issue of transmission was clearly a central concern to the CEGB in the siting of a power station, but this essential link has been lost as a result of the new procedures established after privatisation of the electricity supply industry in 1989.

Since the EIA Directive clearly requires all direct, indirect and secondary effects of a project to be assessed, much hinges on the definition of 'project'. The environmental statement for the Wilton power station refers to the 'overall project' as including the power station and associated developments, such as the transmission lines. In this case it would appear that the project was divided into separate sub-projects, with the environmental impact of each part assessed separately. The complaint argued that it was not appropriate to assess the impact of associated developments in isolation from the main development, including the implications of its siting.

The European Commission agreed with the principle of the complaint, but was unwilling to pursue infringement proceedings against the UK in this case:

> "As a general principle ... combined assessment of the effects of the construction of power plants and of any resultant power lines will be necessary in accordance with the Directive [85/337/EEC] when any such power lines are likely to have a significant impact on the environment."
>
> Letter from EC to CPRE, 26.6.92

This was further clarified in a letter closing the file on this case from the Commission to CPRE (11.11.93):

> "I can confirm that it remains the Commission's view that, as a general principle, when it is proposed to construct a power plant together with any power lines either (a) which will need to be constructed in order to enable the proposed plant to function, or (b) which it is proposed to construct in connection with the proposals to construct the power plant, combined assessment of the effects of the construction of both the plant and the power lines in question will be necessary under Articles 3 and 5 of Directive 85/337/EEC when any such power lines are likely to have a significant impact on the environment."

For some time the question hinged on whether the power lines were required primarily to service the power station. The Government argued that they were not, yet evidence submitted by the National Grid Company to the public inquiry made it quite clear that an agreement had been reached with Teesside Power Limited that the upgrading of the national grid would be made by 1995 to comply with the limited derogation from the transmission standards agreed for a temporary period only by the Office of Electricity Regulation (OFFER). Until that time, a temporary local connection to the national grid has been allowed.

Commission action in this case would have been consistent with precedent which suggested that the splitting of a project should be considered to be contrary to the Directive. With regard to a closely analogous situation, that of the Channel Tunnel Rail Link and Kings Cross Terminal, the Commission said in an article 169 letter to the UK Government:-

> 'The effect of dividing the London-Channel Tunnel project into the rail link on the one hand, and the terminal on the other, leads to the circumvention of Directive 85/337/EEC, since the siting of the rail link in London is no longer capable of being assessed and - for instance by the choice of another site for the terminal - its effects minimized during the consideration of the rail link route.
>
> "Terminal and link are, because of the impact of the choice of the terminal site on the link, or the link on the site, indissociable. The intention to assess the link once the assessment of the impact of the terminal is over does not, therefore make acceptable the assessment of the terminal within the Private Bill procedure, which failed, contrary to Article 3 of the Directive, to take into account the effects of its siting on the choice of the rail link."
>
> (letter from Environment Commissioner to UK Government, 17 October 1991)

This was precisely the point being made over the NGC power lines proposals and the Teesside power station at Wilton. They are indissociable; the power lines would not be required were it not for the new power station, and the location of the power station is fundamental to the routes of the power lines. The same is true for the new gas pipeline and other associated developments. The impact of the power station on the environment is at least the sum of the impacts of the constituent, consequential and associated parts, and may be more than the sum (synergistic). It is the clearly stated aim of the Directive to address all of these effects at the time of the main project proposal:-

> "A description (1) of the likely significant effects of the proposed project on the environment resulting from....the existence of the project......"

"(1) This description should cover the direct effects and any indirect, secondary, cumulative, short, medium and long-term, permanent and temporary, positive and negative effects of the project."

(85/337/EEC, Annex III)

The complainant, the Council for the Protection of Rural England (CPRE), argued at the public inquiry into the power lines that the unacceptable visual intrusion which the proposed transmission lines would bring should have been foreseen at a much earlier stage. CPRE argued that these impacts were unacceptable and urged the Inspector to reject the applications for consent on visual grounds. In so doing, CPRE also urged the Inspector to comment on the procedures which brought about this situation, and that the Inspector should not feel obliged to grant consent for the power lines simply because consent for the power station had already been granted and it was already being built. Teesside Power Ltd neither had to demonstrate the full environmental implications of the siting and development implications of the power station, nor to bear the full economic and environmental costs. Limits on the costs that can be passed by the NGC to individual generating projects mean that NGC are likely to seek to develop the cheapest options, since additional costs to minimise the environmental impact will have to be borne by NGC and not the 'polluter' - Teesside Power Ltd..

NGC are faced with an apparent fait accompli of having to connect a generator to the national grid, but neither they, nor anyone else, has the opportunity to object to the siting of the power station requiring connection because the power line implications of the power station were excluded from the EIA and consideration under the existing consent procedures. Had they been included they may have tipped the balance as to whether consent should have been granted at an alternative site closer to existing grid capacity.

This complaint seems to present a good case that the present procedures for consent approval in the Electricity Supply Industry

(ESI) run counter to both the spirit and letter of the EIA Directive. The fact that the Commission has taken no action does not mean there is not a case to answer. The Commission inevitably operates in a highly political arena and this complaint may have suffered by its temporal proximity to other highly publicised and controversial actions at the time (Twyford Down, Oxleas Wood). The fact that the Commission has decided not to pursue legal action does not mean that there was not a case of infringement, the Commission is under no obligation to do so and there is little chance of legal remedy against the Commission (see Alfons Lutticke GmbH et al v Commission Case 48/65 (1966) ECR 19 and Lord Bethell v Commission Case 246/81 (1982) ECR 2277). Legal action by the Commission would probably have meant that the Electricity Act 1989 would have to be amended, or at the very least the Electricity EIA Regulations. The Commission's statement of principle above, however, implies that the UK will have to amend its implementation of EIA for power plants and power lines if it is not to face possible legal action in future. Needless to say, the Inspector's report of the power lines inquiry, which ended in December 1992, is eagerly awaited.

Assessment of all aspects of an electricity generating project would not remove the need for detailed EIA at the transmission line proposal stage, but it would mean that an overall assessment would be made of the main environmental implications of associated developments, including the likely requirements and environmental implications of new transmission lines and system upgrades at the time of a power station proposal. Such considerations did occur before the separation of functions and assessment procedures on privatisation, but no longer.

One way the Government could repair this problem would be to amend the Electricity EIA Regulations along the following lines (CPRE, 1993):

'Page 2, Regulation 3, insert:

"(3) Pursuant to paragraph 1 (a) above an environmental statement shall include information regarding the overall implications for, and impact of, power transmission lines and other infrastructure associated with the generating station where these are likely to have significant effects on the environment." [1]

This would ensure that power station proponents were forced to consider transmission implications of their proposals and that they would form part of the EIA and of any subsequent public inquiry. It would begin to reduce the difficulties which arise over the definition of projects and programmes.

Case Study 2: Assessing the environmental impact of roads

A complaint was registered with the European Commission against the UK Secretary of State for Transport in September 1991 concerning the implementation of the EC Directive on Environmental Impact Assessment (85/337/EEC) with respect to road proposals (CPRE, 1991d).

The complaint argued that UK implementation of Environmental Impact Assessment (EA) for roads fails to comply with the requirements of the EIA Directive. In particular, that the Departmental guidance on EIA - the Manual of Environmental Appraisal (1983) and the Departmental Standard on Environmental Assessment (HD 18/88) - was inadequate, out of date, and fails to incorporate fundamental requirements of the EIA Directive.

The key concerns were:-

- the inadequacy and limitations of the 'Framework' approach used by the Department of Transport in presenting environmental information, with its over-emphasis on user groups and policies likely to be affected by the road rather than on the wider environment;

- the inadequate definition of 'project' which results in the splitting of proposed routes into small sections for consent and assessment purposes, without a strategic assessment of the whole proposal. Linked to this is the failure to require proper assessment of indirect, secondary and other effects, as required under article 3 and Annex III of the Directive.

This is an important complaint because it is not individual project specific; it is a generic complaint over the principle of poor application. It is therefore more far reaching and more difficult for the UK Government to dismiss.

While article 5 of the Directive provides Member States with a degree of discretion regarding the information specified in Annex III that is relevant to a given consent procedure and to the specific characteristics of a particular project or type of project (art. 5(1)(a)), and that a developer may reasonably be required to compile (art. 5(1)(b)), the complaint argued that the Secretary of State for Transport had failed to exercise this discretion appropriately in the case of road proposals.

Article 5 (1) arguably requires the information specified in Annex III where it is relevant to the specific characteristics of the proposal or 'type of project' and at some stage during the assessment process; Member State discretion over the latter being exercised over the stage at which it is relevant. Article 5 (1) also refers to the provision of information 'having regard inter alia to current knowledge and methods of assessment'. It is not unreasonable to expect the information referred to in Annex III to be supplied by the proponent of the scheme. Article 5 (2) refers to the minimum information to be provided by the developer, which must include "the data required to identify and assess the main effects which the project is likely to have on the environment." Arguably, Annex III indicates the type of data necessary for such an identification and assessment.

The European Commission investigated the complaint that the Secretary of State for Transport had failed to establish sufficient procedures, methodologies or criteria for assessing the effects on the environment of road proposals to comply with the EIA Directive (85/337/EEC) in full. The procedures and guidance followed by Member States in implementing the Directive are as important as the relevant legislation, to the extent that even if the legislation appears to comply with the Directive, ie there has been correct transposition, in practice the Member State may be in breach of its requirements, ie there is poor application.

The UK Department of Transport published its revised Manual of Environmental Appraisal in July 1993 (see Chapter 5). However, this new guide - Volume 11 of the Design Manual for Roads and Bridges - although bringing some welcome improvements to the assessment of detailed aspects of the environment when a road scheme is proposed still fails to address the wider and more fundamental issues, namely the splitting of road projects into small schemes and its lack of attention to avoidance of impacts rather than mitigation. The Commission is continuing to investigate the complaint. However, a similar case from Germany (Case C-396/92: brought by Bund Naturschutz and others) has been referred to the European Court of Justice by the Bavarian Higher Regional Administrative Court; the UK Government has indicated that it will make an intervention arguing that the separation of road schemes into small sections does comply with the EIA Directive.

The question to come before the European Court (in March 1994) was:

"Is the concept of 'project' in Articles 1,3 and 4 of, and Annex I (7) to, the Directive to be understood as meaning, in its application to motorways and express roads, that the environmental impact

(a) is to be assessed solely for the section of a road link for which development consent has been sought,   or........

(b) in addition to the area covered by that section, for the road link as a whole?"

The outcome of this case is likely to have some bearing on the UK complaint outlined above, although it goes further than simply the splitting of schemes into small sections. This issue was also addressed in an application for judicial review by Surrey County Council in November 1993 over the UK Government's proposed widening of, and link roads to, the M25 motorway. Mr Justice MacPhearson, although rejecting application for judicial review on the grounds that as no ES yet existed the application was premature, said that the Government should require EIA for the whole project, not simply individual sections (see Chapter 9 for more details).

Establishing SEA in legislation

We have seen above the difficulties presented by limiting EIA in legislation to projects only. In practice projects are not always as discretely defined as required for legal definitions. Legislation for EIA over the last 25 years throughout the world has, however, focused largely on project EIA, even where some provision has been made for more strategic assessment. While undoubtedly beneficial, project EIA alone lacks the flexibility of a tiered approach because many of the most important or irreversible decisions have already been made at previous stages, not least those on alternatives. Accordingly, project EIA alone frequently results in little more than appraisal of irreversible impacts rather than securing avoidance from the beginning. On the other hand a tiered EIA system offers a fluid and coherent approach to considering environmental effects in decisions from the very earliest stages.

EIA generally can be incorporated into national legislation in two major ways:

> i) the sectoral approach: land use and resource planning is divided into various policy sectors, for example roads, water, energy, consent for development projects. Separate provisions are made for EIA under each sector. This is a common approach to environmental protection and can be seen, for instance, in the United Kingdom, Sweden, and Kenya.

ii) the framework approach: EIA is established through a single body of legislation applicable to all or many policy sectors, ensuring consistent requirements throughout. Examples of this approach include NEPA and CEQA in the US, New Zealand and, ironically, the EC Directive which, while establishing a framework, is often implemented in Member States in a sectoral manner.

While the sectoral approach may be effective in establishing project EIA in particular, the framework approach appears to be more amenable to establishing a tiered EIA system. Many countries with existing sectoral legislation will tend to introduce EIA in a sectoral way. This can result in many pieces of often secondary legislation with varying EIA requirements, unless real efforts are made to ensure consistency. In the UK, for example, there is marked variation between the EIA requirements and procedures for projects that require development consent (planning permission) from local authorities and, for example, major roads and motorways. There is yet further variation in the implementation of EIA for forestry, energy and agricultural projects. Incorporating SEA into sectoral legislation may therefore result in a plethora of varying standards. This does not mean that SEA or a comprehensive tiered system cannot be established under a sectoral approach, but it is likely to need considerably more care to ensure consistency.

Because of its comprehensive nature, the framework approach tends better to favour the inclusion of environmental information into early decision-making processes and, therefore, is more readily able to address strategic environmental assessment. Most importantly, it allows SEA and project EIA to be covered by a unified set of legislation.

For instance, New Zealand's Resource Management Act establishes a comprehensive land use and resource planning structure which incorporates consistent EIA throughout. NEPA and CEQA each provide one set of standards for EIA regardless of sector and decision level. The EC Directive 85/337/EEC, properly amended and implemented, could also establish such a comprehensive framework (Cerny and Sheate, 1992; CPRE, 1992).

Even where EIA legislation does not reach into strategic decision levels the inclusion of cumulative effects in project EIA can enable some of the wider impacts of a proposed project to be addressed which might otherwise have been covered by SEA had it been in place. While cumulative effects assessment is in no way an alternative to SEA it can mean that an individual project is no longer considered in isolation.

SEA in the EC

During 1991/92 a Draft Proposal for an EC Directive on SEA was prepared by the European Commission, although it never achieved formal status. Following the Edinburgh Summit of EC Heads of State in December 1992 the EC withdrew the Draft Proposal ostensibly in favour of amending the present Directive on project EIA to take on aspects of SEA (Cerny & Sheate, 1992), but in fact largely because of the opposition of various Member States including the UK. Moreover, the present political reality means progress on SEA is likely to be very slow indeed. There may even be threats to weaken the present project EIA Directive following the difficulties in ratifying the Maastricht Treaty on European Union and the emphasis on 'subsidiarity' (the principle of taking action only at the most appropriate level) as a way of minimising the EC involvement in different policy areas.

Several characteristics of the Draft SEA Proposal are worth examining. First, although it took the form of a separate directive rather than amendment of the existing Directive, it followed a very similar structure to that of the project EIA Directive. A general obligation was to be placed upon the Member States to ensure that certain types of policies, plans and programmes (PPPs) (for example, transport and energy policies) listed in the annex would undergo EIA, while Member States have the option of requiring EIA for other types of PPPs not listed in the annex. Directive 85/337/EEC uses the same sort of annex system to determine the types of projects to which it applies, although this has generated its own difficulties (see Chapter 4).

Second, neither the present directive nor the Draft Proposal required the creation of new institutions to oversee the EIA process. Rather, the EIA requirements were meant to supplement the existing planning and authorization procedures of the Member States.

Third, the scope of the Draft Proposal was broad, and included the secondary, cumulative, and synergistic effects of the policy, plan, or programme, as well as its main alternatives. The scope also included the compatibility of the PPP with national and regional environmental goals and with the actions taken in furtherance of those goals.

Fourth, the requirements for publication and public consultation were similar under the Draft Proposal and the Directive. Significantly, the public has no formal opportunity under either the Draft SEA Proposal or Directive 85/337/EEC to be consulted prior to publication of the environmental assessment report.

Finally, the Draft Proposal included a number of exemptions and would have applied only where appropriate PPPs exist. It would not have applied to PPPs approved according to national or, in appropriate cases, regional cabinet procedures which incorporate an environmental assessment report in consultation with the Minister responsible for the environment. Furthermore, a PPP may have been exempted if (a) implementation will not give rise to significant environmental effects, or (b) any significant environmental effects would have been adequately assessed and addressed at other stages of the planning process.

The current draft proposal (as of 1993/4) is a greatly watered-down affair, and no longer refers to SEA as such but instead is supposed to establish "some common provisions to integrate environmental protection requirements in the decision making process for certain economic and other sectors". It is, however, at least set in the context of sustainable development, but will no doubt still face the hostility of the UK and probably Germany and Denmark.

The EC's five-year review of the EIA Directive has provided the basis for the European Commission to come forward with amendments for improving the Directive. Some commentators (Sheate & Cerny, 1993; Cerny and Sheate, 1992; CPRE, 1992) have argued that the present Directive can and should be amended to take on SEA, ensuring a single body of EC law rather than separate Directives with the potential for inconsistency in standards and implementation (and, indeed, translation). Nowhere, where both SEA and project EIA both exist, has SEA been introduced in legislation separately from project EIA. One body of law is crucial to achieving an effective tiered EIA system. Suggestions that SEA requires different techniques (Deansley et al, 1993) to project EIA and therefore requires separate legislation rather misses the point about legislating for EIA. EIA legislation should lay down clear procedures to be followed (EIA is essentially a procedural tool). Such procedures are generally similar and have common features, eg scoping, identification and assessment of impacts, public participation, at all levels of decision making. The techniques and methods used in implementing those procedures also have some common features although there may also be differences. The techniques used, however, have little to do with the legislation; legislation rarely specifies techniques that must be adopted to meet the procedural requirements of the legislation. Nor should it, since techniques and methodologies may change rapidly over time. That would normally be left to Government guidance.

United Kingdom

A report published by the UK Government, 'Policy Appraisal and the Environment' (UK DoE, 1991a) highlights the conceptual difficulties governments may face in taking on board the environment wholeheartedly in the decision-making process. 'Appraisal' has been seen in some quarters as an alternative to SEA. But they are not, by all accounts, one and the same thing.

Appraisal is being promoted by the UK Government as a way of taking environmental considerations into account in policy formulation. Its use is advised for local authority development and land use plans and for policies formulated by government departments, although there have been few examples of the latter. Appraisal would appear to be much more about identifying the impacts of a particular policy or proposal, so that those impacts are known (taken into account), but it does not necessarily result in any modification of the proposal. Strategic environmental assessment is a much more iterative process, and therefore should be applied at the earliest opportunity, from the very start of the planning and design process (Sheate, 1992a). As impacts are identified, these are fed back into the design so that impacts can be minimised or removed. EIA is much more likely to result in changes to the original proposal, and should look at alternative ways of achieving the original objective. Appraisal is more about identifying the costs and impacts of a particular option that has already been chosen, than about choosing an option which has the least impact. Appraisal can, perhaps, be more readily applied to existing policies whereas SEA is best and most easily incorporated into objectives-led policy formulation (see Chapter 11). SEA is therefore naturally more reliant upon the establishment of new approaches to policy formulation.

It seems that the UK Government is somewhat uneasy about SEA. By encouraging policy appraisal rather than SEA the Government is able to distance policy considerations from EIA at the project level. SEA, ideally, requires a tiered approach which connects policy assessment with plan, programme and project assessment. Policy appraisal keeps EIA confined to the project level and militates against the need to introduce objectives-led formulation of policy. It is vitally important that EIA is seen as the best way of incorporating the environment into the decision-making process, rather than the less rigorous appraisal. Semantics apart, the chances of achieving an environmentally sustainable future through the application of appraisal rather than SEA are likely to be considerably less. A recent report (November 1993) published by the UK Department of the Environment, however, to provide guidance to local authorities on carrying out policy appraisal on development plans has taken on board best practice and would appear to be suggesting something much more akin to SEA proper, even though the Government is determined not to call it that (see Chapter 11).

United States of America

Strategic Environmental Assessment under NEPA

NEPA requires that environmental impact assessment be applied not only to federal actions at the project level, but also to programmes, rules and regulations, plans, policies, procedures, and legislative proposals. NEPA's term for these more broadly scoped documents is "programmatic environmental impact statement" (PEIS). There are no separate regulations governing the preparation of the PEIS as opposed to an ordinary EIS; rather, agencies are expected to use their best judgment on the content of the PEIS, taking into consideration its intrinsically broader nature (Webb & Sigal, 1992).

In general, PEISs are prepared for federal actions that are related geographically, generically, or by stage of technological development. Although PEISs were rarely prepared during the 1970s and early 1980s while the principles of NEPA were developing, PEISs have more recently been used in a growing variety of circumstances. The most frequently prepared types of PEISs fall into the following categories:

- Analyses of proposed regulations;
- Programmes for flood or pest control;
- Waste disposal programs;
- Area-wide and technology development programmes;
- Resource management programmes;
- Water development; and
- Policies for rates and permits

California

Although CEQA's basic procedures largely mirror NEPA, CEQA's extension of EIA to policies, plans, and programmes bears elaboration. This extension was accomplished largely through the broadening of the definition of 'project' to include PPPs proposed by public agencies and General Plans formulated by local authorities (Selmi, 1984).

CEQA embraces PPPs through its wide definition of project and applies to any project that may have a significant adverse effect on the environment. A 'project' is any activity directly undertaken, supported, or approved by a public agency - a definition embracing almost any conceivable action taken by a public agency. Furthermore, CEQA requires that EIA be carried out as early as possible in the planning process to enable environmental considerations to influence decisions.

The CEQA Guidelines make provision for the preparation of programme environmental impact reports ('programme EIRs'). A programme EIR may be prepared when an agency proposes a series of activities that are linked geographically or are parts in a logical chain of intended actions. Programme EIRs may also apply to the issuance of rules or regulations governing a continuing programme or to a series of individual activities authorized by the same agency and having generally similar environmental effects. In addition, California's planning laws run parallel to, and, in many ways, complement CEQA. Each local government must formulate and maintain General Plans which articulate development goals. These plans are subject to CEQA requirements, and the public must be consulted before a General Plan is adopted.

Programme EIRs must include the same components as project EIRs, including, among other things, a description of the local and regional environment, the existing infrastructure, and current levels of use; a description of the proposal and a full discussion of alternative proposals and possible mitigation measures; and an evaluation of the proposal's likely effects on the environment, including the increased stress which may result from population growth.

Two additional components exclusive to programme EIRs address the concept of sustainable development: first, a discussion of the relationship between local, short-term uses of the environment and long-term productivity; second, the identification of any significant irreversible changes that would result from the proposed action. Under the former, the EIR must discuss future uses of the environment which are precluded by the proposal and explain why the action is advisable at present. The latter involves discussion of the proposed uses of non-renewable resources and their effects on future generations (Bass, 1990).

It has been recognized by both NEPA and CEQA that damage often occurs incrementally from a variety of small sources which individually might seem insignificant. An EIR is therefore required where the incremental effects of an individual project are significant when viewed in connection with the related effects of past, present, and reasonably foreseeable future projects. The inclusion of cumulative impacts of this kind can accomplish some of the purposes of EIA of PPPs even at the project level. Study of cumulative impacts tends to broaden the view of the proponent by ensuring consideration of the regional consequences of the proposal. This can provide a partial safety net for an inadequate or nonexistent programme EIR.

In addition, NEPA and CEQA encourage the use of 'tiering', under which broad EIRs of general plans feed subsequent, more specific project EIRs. Through the EIA or the initial study, the lead authority determines whether a project proposal falls within the scope of an existing programme EIR. If so, the lead agency may adopt measures mentioned in the programme EIR that mitigate or avoid significant effects. Even if the project proposal is not within the scope of a programme EIR, the lead authority may draw upon information and analysis contained in it. Tiering has been shown in the US to save time and effort by avoiding adverse impacts and by preventing duplication.

Canada

Ostensibly, the language of the Guidelines Order (see Chapter 4) encompassed EIA of PPPs: EIA must begin "as early in the planning process as possible, and before irrevocable decisions are taken." Furthermore, the interplay between the application of the Guidelines Order and the definition of "proposal" is significant. The Guidelines applied to any proposal that was to be undertaken directly by an initiating department, or that may have an environmental effect on an area of federal responsibility, or that was sponsored by federal funds. A "proposal" is any initiative, undertaking, or activity for which the Government has a decision-making responsibility. The formulation by state authorities of policies, plans, and programmes would certainly be caught by these two provisions. Indeed, the courts and the Government had concurred that the Guidelines Order covered PPPs (Schrecker, 1991).

However, until the Guidelines Order was made legally binding by the courts, the Government's application of EIA to PPPs had been erratic. Many PPPs that would have important environmental consequences, such as cuts in passenger rail services, were not subject to EIA (Hunt, 1990). Moreover, having been surprised by the sudden enforceability of the Guidelines Order, government departments scrambled to revise their procedures for SEA. The uncertainty under the Guidelines Order highlighted the need for a solid statutory base for EIA in Canada, but the Canadian Environmental Assessment Act 1992 (CEAA) may create as many problems as it solves. The scope of the CEAA would include only projects of a "physical" nature. In other words, PPPs, which very often do not involve specific construction plans, may be excluded altogether. The CEAA contemplates that EIA of PPPs will take place at the cabinet level, reinforced by the House of Commons Standing Committee on the Environment which can request Ministers to explain the environmental implications of a Government policy. This, however, runs the same dangers as policy appraisal in the UK: the lack of consistency between decision making levels, the absence of effective tiering, and the deferral of introducing policy formulation procedures which incorporate environmentally sustainable objectives.

New Zealand

In October, 1991 New Zealand revamped its resource planning and EIA procedures by enacting the Resource Management

151

Act (the Act) which consolidated New Zealand's resource planning law under the common purpose "to promote the sustainable management of natural and physical resources."

Rather than provide separately for EIA, it is a constant theme throughout the statute. Regional policy statements, for example, promote sustainable development by providing an overview of resource management issues in the region. Each regional policy statement must include, among other things, the environmental effects anticipated from the implementation of the policies and the reasons for choosing particular policies and implementation procedures. The same pattern of requirements applies to territorial, coastal, and district policies and plans, as well as to regional rules and regulations.

Guided by the concept of sustainable development, the Act's planning structure is intended to be comprehensive and consistent, exemplifying the tiered approach. At the top tier, national policy statements articulate general policies applicable to the nation as a whole. The regional authorities then focus these policies on narrower issues relevant to their jurisdictions. The territorial authorities, in turn, apply regional plans to more specific, local issues. The policy and planning statements of the national, coastal, and local authorities should be consistent, each tier conforming to the one above. Significant inconsistencies or disputes are referred to a Planning Tribunal.

New Zealand, therefore, has provided not only for EIA but for a unified and comprehensive planning structure, centred around resource management. In taking on SEA, the logical necessity to take a new approach to policy formulation has not been ducked; rather it has been taken on wholeheartedly. In legislative terms, the Resource Management Act provides a fine example of the integration of environmental concerns into decision-making.

Chapter 11

S.E.A. IN PRACTICE

Introduction

It is often argued by politicians that there is little experience of strategic environmental assessment or that it is difficult to see how SEA would fit in with policy formulation. However, that argument increasingly can be seen as having little foundation in fact.

Project level EIA alone cannot achieve environmentally sustainable policies; where there is only project EIA it often strains to accommodate those issues that are properly the concern of higher level EIAs, and therefore often fails to varying degrees. Without SEA the relative role that eg road transport should play in meeting environmentally sustainable transport policy objectives cannot be determined.

As we have seen in previous chapters, with a tiered approach to EIA, stretching from the project, through strategic levels of programme, plan and policy, the difficulty over definition of project is removed. The distinction becomes academic, once programme EIA is in place.

But the real value of SEA is that it enables informed choices to be made, at the earliest decision-making levels and when it matters most, as to the relative role different options and development patterns should play within an overall sectoral policy. Ideally, that policy needs to be objectives-led, with the over-riding aim of achieving environmental sustainability. The key, therefore, to applying effective SEA at the policy level and below is the development of objectives-led policy (and plan and programme) formulation.

Figure 11.1 illustrates how this might be achieved and the point at which, in the policy process, strategic environmental assessment should arise.

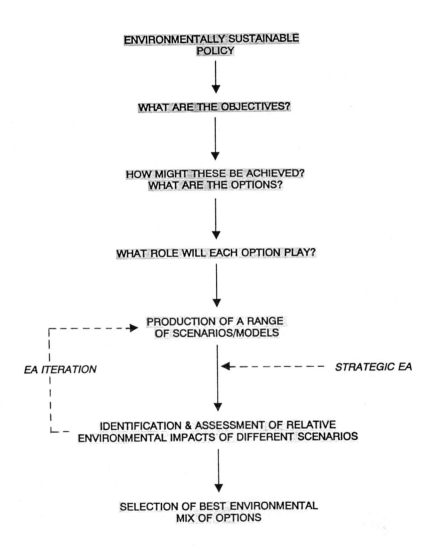

Generalised objectives-led policy formulation
(after Sheate, 1992)

Figure 11.1 Generalised objectives-led policy formulation (after Sheate, 1992cc).

Objectives

Central to applying strategic environmental assessment in any sector should be clearly identified objectives for the overall policy set within the overall aim of establishing an environmentally sustainable policy. Objectives may be quantitative targets or qualitative statements of intent. Even qualitative statements could be focused by setting quantitative targets. For example, in the transport sector, an objective 'reduce the need to travel' could be expressed in a more quantitative way by 'reduce miles travelled by x%'. Quantitative targets will never, however, wholly replace qualitative objectives. It may be that the setting of objectives and targets could be seen as a two stage process, with the initial setting of general, more qualitative objectives and the subsequent setting of targets, eg specific goals within a certain time. A general objective to maximise opportunities for cycling may require the setting of a target of reducing cyclist accidents by x%. Figure 11.2 (Sheate, 1992c) illustrates this as occurring simultaneously because it may not always be appropriate to imply that all general objectives should then be refined by specific targets. In Figure 11.2, a mix of target-based objectives and general qualitative objectives has been suggested.

Figure 11.2 suggests a number of possible objectives; there could easily be many more or fewer. It is already commonplace to establish targets for safety purposes and accident reduction, and there are examples of setting other targets, for instance, for increasing the modal split for cycling of total journeys to work, eg an objective of achieving 6% of the total journey to work modal split in an urban area by the year 2000 (TEST, 1992). Others have identified a wide range of possible targets for securing environmentally sustainable transport policies (Roberts et al, 1992). Increasingly objectives may be based on international agreements, eg 'reduce CO_2 levels by x%'. This objective could be expressed as 'stabilisation of CO_2 emissions to 1990 levels by 2000'.

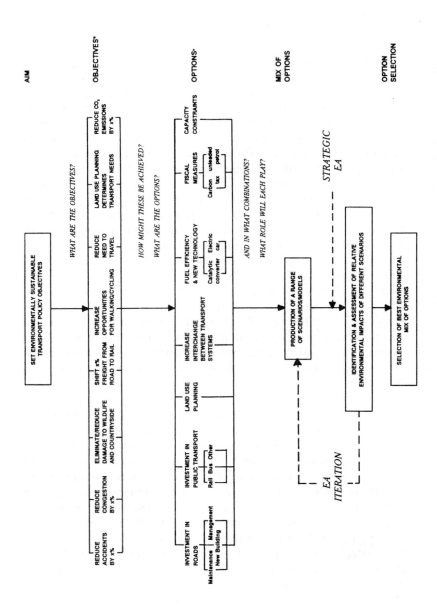

Figure 11.2 Strategic environmental assessment in objectives-led transport policy formulation. (Reproduced from Sheate, W.R., Project Appraisal 7 (3), September 1992; 10 Watford Close, Guildford, Surrey, GU1 2EP, UK)

Options

Once objectives have been established, the next task in policy formulation, as Figure 11.1 indicates, should be to identify the possible options for achieving these objectives. Figure 11.2 identifies some examples for the transport sector, which might include investment in road, rail, new technology, provision of airport capacity, the use of fiscal measures and the role of land use planning in ensuring that the provision of transport infrastructure and facilities complements land use priorities, rather than drives them. For example, the construction of out-of-town shopping centres creates significant additional demands for travel by car, and has implications for the viability of shopping facilities in urban areas where additional and specific journeys may not otherwise have been required. Roads can shift the overall balance of accessibility and market forces in an area, resulting in wholly new pressures for development as well as having large and direct effects on the environment. Land use planning, therefore, offers real opportunities for securing long-term environmental sustainability by addressing the fundamental questions about where development occurs and how that development is best served by transport infrastructure. The energy implications of different development scenarios, through their transport implications, should be central. Investment in roads, on the other hand, could take the form of investment in aspects other than simply new road building, eg traffic management schemes or on-line improvements. Fiscal measures could be in the form of taxes, eg a carbon tax, or in the form of price incentives, such as a reduced price for unleaded petrol compared to leaded. Capacity constraints, eg existing road or airport capacity, could be seen as a positive tool for managing transport provision. Rather than indicating a need to increase capacity such constraints could be seen as incentives for finding alternative solutions.

A transport policy based on environmental principles would also seek to maximise inter-change between transport systems. For instance, new railway stations should be connected to local communities by appropriate bus or other public transport provision if objectives such as reducing congestion, emissions and the need to travel by car are to be achieved.

Strategic Environmental Assessment

Having identified the range of possible options the next stage in the formulation of an environmentally sustainable policy should be the production of a range of scenarios or models (Figure 11.1), which take as their basis varying roles for, or levels of investment in, the different options identified. With transport policy, for instance, there could be a number of different combinations of fiscal measures and road investment, public transport and fuel efficiency, incorporating some or none of the different options. It is at this stage that strategic environmental assessment should be incorporated into the policy formulation process. By applying the principles of EIA to the various scenarios the relative environmental impacts of each scenario can be identified and assessed. In so doing there will be iteration into the process of identifying scenarios until the selection of a best environmental mix of options emerges. That mix of options will be the mix which enables the objectives to be met in the most environmentally sustainable way.

Figure 11.2 illustrates the principle of applying SEA at the transport policy level, but a tiered approach to EIA necessitates its application to subsequent decision levels down to and including the project level. For instance, if a level of road investment has been identified during the policy formulation and SEA process, the question needs to be asked as to what proportion should go on building new roads, traffic management or on-line improvements.

Where a national plan/programme for road building by government exists (in the UK this is the Trunk Roads Programme) it is essential that road proposals should only enter the programme after EIA has occurred, so that only those roads identified as being the best environmental option go forward. EIA will have allowed a choice between new roads and other alternative forms of road investment and between alternative modes. However, it needs to be stressed that the value of a tiered approach is that just because a decision has been taken at an earlier stage that x% should be invested in road improvements/building does not mean that that has to occur even in the face of evidence at a subsequent, more detailed EIA level that another alternative solution would be more environmentally sustainable. In deciding which road proposals should go into a national road building programme, the question of whether an alternative mode might not better meet the objectives should not be excluded. A tiered approach to EIA enables a greater degree of refinement at each stage from the policy level downwards, and the existence of a road in a roads programme should not prevent it from being thrown out if evidence comes forward that an alternative approach would be more appropriate or, indeed, a road building option being added. The iterative nature of EIA demands the possibility that such feedback loops should exist between the different tiers.

In the public transport field SEA could be included with considerable effect in the preparation of public transport plans by local, regional and other relevant authorities; in annual financial allocations; and in the formulation and integration of land use plans with transport planning.

Procedure and methods

One of the arguments frequently raised by policy-makers is that SEA would be difficult to carry out in practice, especially at the policy level. How, it is often asked, can EIA be incorporated on a statutory basis into a process which is essentially fluid and continuous? That may be a natural response where the experience has been only of project EIA applied to consent procedures and, however unfortunately, often seen as 'bolted on' to an existing process. EIA, however, is actually a natural adjunct to a dynamic process such as policy formulation because, as we have seen, iteration is inherent.

The identification of the best environmental mix of options is the point at which the equivalent to an environmental report or statement should be produced, which should provide the focus for public participation. Public participation should be an integral element of environmental assessment in general (Sheate, 1991) and therefore when applied at the strategic level offers much-needed opportunities for public involvement in early decision-making. Such opportunities may already exist, for instance on draft land use plans, but in other cases they may not. In the UK, for example, there is no public involvement in the establishment of the national Trunk Roads Programme. The reason for public opposition to many road proposals is often because there have been no opportunities for public input before route options are proposed. What specific methods and procedures, however, should be adopted in order to carry out SEA in the transport sector? First, SEA is already being undertaken in many countries and to varying extents and in various sectors (eg USA, New Zealand, Canada, Netherlands), and draws heavily on methodologies used in project-level assessment. In essence, similar methods can be used, but the detail involved will be different: it is essential to recognise that a tiered approach to EIA requires the assessment at a particular decision-making level to address only that detail which is appropriate to it.

Crucial to SEA being effective is the inclusion of the findings of the SEA process at the most appropriate place in the planning and decision-making procedure. The importance of public participation has already been identified, and the results of the SEA should be included in public consultation on any draft policy, plan or programme. The outcome of the assessment and the consultation process should then be taken into account in reaching a decision to approve or proceed with the action in question (Lee and Lewis, 1991). Post-decision monitoring should then follow to ensure that the outcome is consistent with that anticipated by the SEA process, and to enable appropriate modifications to the process where necessary.

The nature and extent of public participation will depend on the level of decision-making, who the 'public' are identified as being for the purposes of the consultation and the time scales involved.

For example, the participation of the general public may not always be feasible if the time scale is very frequent, eg an annual review of financial allocation to transport modes. Consultations may need to be limited to elected representatives and/or statutory and voluntary (public interest) organisations in such situations, although the general public should not be excluded.

Methods for carrying out SEA need not be substantially different from project level EIA. The tasks involved are unlikely to be very dissimilar but, as Figure 11.1 illustrates, should focus on objectives and options. There will still be a need, as in project EIA, for base line environmental data, but at SEA levels this will be of a much more general nature.

The identification and assessment of significant environmental impacts will be enabled by the scenario approach suggested. For each scenario similar methods of assessment to those used at project level EIA can be utilised, albeit in a simplified and more 'broad brush' way.

The use of matrices may well be appropriate for summarising the findings of the SEA for each scenario and/or option, and to aid decisions over the best environmental mix of options.

In most cases of policy formulation the proponent is also the competent authority. Independent scrutiny and public participation are therefore even more crucial than at the project level where the two roles are more often separated. Independent scrutiny, eg by an EIA agency, should ensure compliance with the requirements of the legislation (or guidelines if not legislated).

Transport

In the UK, examples of the use of SEA in the transport sector are coming forward, as the search for solutions to the diversity of transport problems settles on the vital mechanism of EIA.

There have, for instance, been SEA studies carried out for a number of public transport plans in urban areas in the UK (Lewis, 1990; Taylor, 1990), illustrating clearly the feasibility and value of its application. Below, some examples of appropriate methods and types of data are suggested for use in transport SEA (Lee and Lewis, 1991):-

Accidents

Accident rate data, data on changes in traffic volumes and modal mix;

Severance

Areas identified where significant changes, population size affected;

Noise

Noise characteristics of vehicles, change in traffic volumes and mix allow assessment of broad changes in noise levels;

Vibration

Generally localised and therefore unlikely to be highly significant in SEA, but potential should be noted;

Use of resources

Expected change in traffic volumes and mix, specific energy consumption ratios for each mode, land take, aggregate requirements;

Air pollution

Standard emission ratios for each mode, predicted changes in traffic volume, mix and average speeds, CO_2 levels;

Visual impacts

Broad assessment of overall scale and key physical characteristics, land take and characteristics of receiving environment;

Historical, nature conservation

Broad assessment of impacts on recognised archaeological sites and general areas of importance (designated and non-designated).

The transport sector in the UK is now in desperate need of SEA and, given the international priorities on environmentally sustainable development now being set as a result of the United Nations Conference on the Environment and Development (UNCED, 1992), the application of SEA assumes even greater significance and urgency. International agreements and treaties are now establishing clear targets and objectives for member countries to adhere to. The only systematic way of meeting these objectives is likely to be the incorporation of SEA into the process of policy, especially in this case transport policy, formulation. The imperative now exists, as does the mechanism for achieving it; there is still some way to go to bring the two elements together. It is happening in some countries, albeit sporadically and often inconsistently, but until it happens systematically, internationally-agreed environmental objectives are unlikely to be achieved.

SEA assumes ever greater importance, especially in the transport sector, as the EC Single Market seeks to establish European networks for road, rail and air transport. As governments look to new policy initiatives to solve increasing transport problems, an assessment of their environmental implications becomes essential. In the UK, motorway charging is one such initiative.

Motorway charging

Proposals issued in 1993 (DOT, 1993) by the UK Government for charging for motorway use illustrate well the need for proper

163

assessment of the environmental implications of policy initiatives. Although the Government addressed some of the potential environmental impacts, notably the likely diversion of traffic from motorways to the rest of the road network, there was no systematic assessment of the range of possible impacts, for instance in accordance with the Government's own guidelines for policy formulation laid down in 'Policy Appraisal and the Environment: A Guide for Government Departments' (UK DoE, 1991a) (see later). One would hope to see a separate chapter of a consultation paper devoted to this crucial issue, not least to provide evidence that the procedures in 'Policy Appraisal and the Environment' are in fact being applied to the formulation of Government policy.

Unfortunately, neither were the implications for other policies addressed. Indeed one of the key criticisms is the way in which the proposals came forward in isolation from an overall and objectives-led strategic transport policy, as suggested above. It is worth looking at this example in some detail since it illustrates the value of a tiered approach to EIA.

The fact that these proposals came forward in the absence of a strategic and environmentally sustainable transport policy is also somewhat ironic given the commitment in the UK Government's consultation paper in 1993 on the National Sustainability Strategy to the definition of "the components and objectives for a sustainable transport policy, looking to both the short and long term". Furthermore, the emphasis within the motorway charging proposals on speeding up the Roads Programme fails to recognise the wider environmental consequences which will result and the further distortion to competition it may cause between road and rail.

Charging for road use

The principle of using price as one mechanism for managing demand for resources, be they water, energy or road space is an accepted one by most environmentalists. The crucial questions to be asked must always be what the objectives of the initiative are meant to be, the form that the charging mechanism will take, how it relates to other relevant policies, and its likely impact on the environment. A charging mechanism is unlikely in itself ever to be the only way in which demand can be managed; it would normally need to be seen as part of a much wider package to manage a resource in a more environmentally sustainable way.

A main objective of the proposals was clearly to raise revenue to extend the motorway widening programme and to encourage further involvement of the private sector. The proposals did not therefore come forward primarily to manage demand for road space. However, even if such a policy were in place, charging for motorway use alone would be unlikely to deliver environmental benefits. Rather, it is likely that it will bring about further environmental damage more rapidly.

The Government implied in its consultation paper that charging for urban roads has no connection with that for interurban roads, illustrating again the lack of any strategic framework for the Government's transport policy. Road pricing (or congestion charging) in urban areas may play a role in managing traffic where it is part of a strategic transport policy. Such road pricing on a geographical, self-contained basis, ie where there is no 'free' road alternative, may be effective in managing demand and helping, in conjunction with other demand management tools and improvements in public transport, to shift passengers from cars to alternative modes. The intention would be to moderate demand by taking traffic off unsuitable roads. The proposals for motorway charging, however, are more likely to lead to an increase in traffic on unsuitable roads as a result of diversion by motorists seeking to avoid paying tolls, whether through physical toll collection, permit or electronic charging.

Diversion

The Government recognised that even at relatively low charges (eg 1.5 pence per mile) there is likely to be a shift of some

10% of traffic from motorways to the rest of the road network in peak periods, and this could be higher in off-peak periods. This is not an insignificant shift in traffic, particularly if it is transferring to inappropriate and often already congested roads. It could also be seen as justification for upgrading the rest of the road network as a result of increasing demand brought about partly by diversion from motorways.

Charging for road-based transport should be about the application of the polluter pays principle. The proposals for motorway charging do not conform to this principle; instead they are fundamentally about whether people are willing to pay to use motorways. The suggestion of permit charging is a particularly active illustration of this where, having purchased a permit, the motorist will have every incentive to use the motorway network as much as possible. The permit is therefore a licence to pollute freely, in complete contradiction to the polluter pays principle.

Legitimate concern by environmental groups over the implications for the rest of the road network are further enhanced by the Government's suggestion that charging might be extended beyond the motorway network to other trunk roads which offer a level of service approaching motorway standard. This could amount to motorway designation by default and ultimately lead to the justification of further upgradings as a consequence. With a permit system in particular, having payed for the permit, motorists would have an incentive to use any road covered by the permit. Additional traffic may therefore be generated as a consequence of permit charging. A useful analogy might be that of paying a flat-rate charge for water (water rates) which removes any incentive for conservation.

Unless the diversion effect described above can be contained by charging on all parts of the road network, charging on one part will simply lead to the displacement of traffic to other parts.

A more appropriate way of implementing the polluter pays principle and of managing demand for road-based travel and hence for road space would be to increase the marginal cost of all road-based travel, in particular by taxing fuel (eg with a carbon/energy tax). The phased increases in fuel taxes announced by the UK Government in 1993 were a step in the right direction, although these are unlikely to fulfil their potential without being part of a wider package of measures. The failure to consider adequately alternatives to the motorway charging proposals exemplifies policy formulation that occurs outside of sustainable development objectives. The extent to which the Government had addressed issues of diversion from the motorway network was an illustration of a bolt-on appraisal of irreversible impacts (having decided the policy for other reasons) rather than the proper inclusion of strategic environmental assessment into policy formulation.

Energy

Strategic environmental assessment could also bring significant benefits to the formulation of energy policies, plans and programmes. This would help to ensure that a clear assessment is made of the total environmental effects of different demand and supply options, in the light of other technical, political and economic priorities and constraints. We have already seen in Chapter 9 the difficulties of defining a power station 'project' and the need for programme EIA.

In the context of recent supply-side proposals in the UK (notably Sizewell B and C, Hinkley C, various wind farm proposals and the 'dash for gas'), many have argued that assessment of the environmental effects of a proposed power station should be integral to the promoter's economic analysis. Two considerations in particular should be given priority. The first is the basic principle of environmental impact assessment that "the best environmental policy consists in preventing the creation of pollution or nuisance at source, rather than subsequently trying to counteract their effects" (EC Directive, 85/337/EEC) The second is that, where mitigation at source cannot be achieved, consideration should be given to the likely effects of alternative ways of achieving the same objective or objectives.

The advantages of renewables over other supply options do not render them unequivocally "good" in environmental terms. There must be a consistent assessment of the environmental advantages and disadvantages of alternative energy policy options.

The best environmental approach would be, therefore, for the Government to apply the principles of strategic environmental assessment, first of all to energy policy overall, so that the role of renewables alongside eg energy conservation, could be determined, followed by an SEA of the current 1500MW target (plan) for renewables by 2000, to identify the environmental effects of different ways of meeting this target. There may be a case for increasing this target, but the larger the target, the greater the need for comprehensive assessment of the different renewable energy options that could be used to meet it. Renewables after all include, among others, wind, biofuels, tidal, wave, incineration and solar. Even the strongest advocates of wind power would not necessarily support massive tidal power developments, for instance, since, at least in the UK, these would invariably have significant environmental effects.

A good example of the application of strategic environmental assessment in the energy sector can be seen in relation to the development of the Netherlands National Structure Plan on Electricity Supply in 1992 (van Eck, 1993). This plan is drawn up by national government and includes the selection of sites for power plants, wind farms and transport facilities as well as decisions on the mix of fuels to be used over the next 20 years life of the plan.

During the SEA process the Minister of Economic Affairs and the Minister of Housing, Physical Planning and Environment acted jointly as competent authority and proponent, although some division of their roles developed as the process continued, the latter becoming more of a competent authority. Proposed sites and transport facilities were checked against the objectives of the Nature Policy Plan and on the basis of impacts on natural resources such as water as well as noise and safety effects. The impact of different fuel mixes was assessed using a number of scenarios: 50% natural gas, 50% coal (this was further broken down into whether the 50% coal was to be powder coal or coal gassification); and 33% natural gas, 33% coal, (gassification), 33% oil gassification. These scenarios were also considered under low and high demand conditions.

The Environmental Impact Statement produced for this SEA was bulky and time consuming, but recognised by all who participated as having been worthwhile. One crucial effect of the EIS was to suggest that the use of coal had to be diminished and restricted to coal gassification largely on the basis of its sulphur dioxide emissions and acidification effects. The EIS also imposed limits on site selection for power plants.

Another example of how SEA could be applied in the energy sector can be seen in Chapter 13, EIA and Pollution Control, with respect to flue gas desulphurisation.

Water

The River Colne Flood Alleviation Study, carried out by Thames Water Rivers Division (prior to water company privatisation) in 1988, and subsequently by the National Rivers Authority (Thames Region), is seen by many as being one of the first and best examples of a strategic (plan level) environmental assessment in the UK (Gardiner, 1992). The study covered a large geographical area and comprised some 60 relatively small-scale individual flood alleviation projects, each being up to £2.5 million in value. The total value of all the works was £12.5 million spread over 20 kilometres of river valley containing 75 kilometres of main river.

One measure of success of the study is that despite the scale of the planned works no public inquiry has been necessary, not least because the public has been consulted as part of the SEA process. An extensive exercise of public consultation at the feasibility stage provided valuable hydrological and environmental information. The National Rivers Authority (Thames Region) is using a similarly strategic approach to EIA with flood management plans and catchment management plans. In 1992 the NRA produced the first floodplain management plan in the UK (initially for the Datchet, Wraysbury, Staines and Chertsey area) which has resulted in significant revision of floodplain policy in the region. Catchment management plans are highly multi-functional and, produced using SEA, can be used to influence local authority development plans.

Policy Appraisal and the Environment

Policy Appraisal and the Environment (PAE) represents the main form of guidance issued by the UK Government for incorporating consideration of the environment into policy formulation. The guidance sets out a suggested methodology for appraising the environmental impact of policies. It is designed for use by Government departments and is seen as applicable to other branches of public service, such as local government.

The UK Government is, however, decidedly schizophrenic when it comes to strategic environmental assessment. On the one hand it is keen to be seen to introducing its own form of 'environmental appraisal' of policies, plans and programmes, but is emphatic that this is not full environmental impact assessment. Certainly, it is not proper SEA, not least because appraisal makes no statutory provision for public participation in the process and there is no requirement in PAE to report publicly on the outcome of the appraisal. Neither is there any requirement for independent scrutiny. Although it urges policy makers to take full account of scientific and public opinions, PAE also stresses that

> "in practice pressures of time and problems of confidentiality may restrict the amount of consultation that can be undertaken." (p7)

Essentially PAE is meant to be complementary to the Treasury guidelines on overall policy appraisal (in economic terms) laid out in 'Economic Appraisal in Central Government'. It is perhaps not surprising, therefore, that PAE focuses on the use of cost benefit techniques and, although it recognises some of the limitations of cost benefit techniques for valuing environmental goods, these are largely forgotten in the detailed discussion.

PAE identifies a series of steps in policy appraisal:

- summarise the policy issue
- list the objectives
- identify the constraints
- specify the options
- identify the costs and benefits
- weigh up the costs and benefits
- test the sensitivity of the options
- suggest the preferred option
- set up any monitoring necessary
- evaluate the policy at a later stage

Apart from there being no mention of public participation, the most notable omission from this list is any concept of sustainable development. In no way does PAE envisage policy formulation being objectives-led from an environmentally sustainable point of view. The objectives referred to in the list are the objectives of the policy, and the options are those options which will meet the objectives of the policy. But the environment is not central to determining either the objectives or the options, and therefore contrasts markedly with the process suggested in Figure 11.1 above. The environmental considerations, although urged to be as early as possible, do not come into the process until the point of identifying the costs and benefits. It is, therefore, essentially a bolt-on process rather than integral to the process of policy formulation. It is less iterative than SEA, though iteration is not entirely absent if the results of the appraisal bring about changes in policy when the policy is next reviewed. Recognising that there are environmental impacts is not sufficient and, even if appraisal does lead to changes in policy at the time of appraisal, the options under consideration are not necessarily appropriate environmental options since the environment is absent from the overall aim of the policy (instead of being environmentally sustainable) and therefore from the setting of the objectives. SEA on the other hand would provide a much better mechanism for avoiding environmental impacts in the first place.

The process suggested in PAE is therefore about appraising policies and/or policy options which themselves are entirely politically derived without any incorporation of sustainable development principles. Therein, it would appear, lies the difficulty the UK Government has with full SEA. SEA would require sustainable development principles to underlie all policy formulation so that the objectives of a policy would have to be environmentally-led. From a politician's point of view, this would seem to remove political freedom for manoeuvre in formulating policy. Since a politician's view is rarely likely to be further than the next general election, this clearly creates a major difficulty if it is seen as essential to be able to modify or manipulate policies according to electoral priorities rather than environmental.

In reality of course, and this has been recognised in those countries where they have accepted the need for SEA, there is still considerable scope for political direction in policy formulation even when the environment is central to policy objectives setting. After all, social and economic factors have been central to policy formulation for many years, but that has not removed political pluralism in formulating policy. There is rarely only one way in which a set of objectives, even environmental, can be delivered. There will always be an important role for political decision making; all the more so where environmental considerations are concerned because it is so difficult, if not impossible, to quantify many environmental parameters. Political decisions as to how important some environmental factors should be will always be essential.

Another difficulty with PAE is that it focuses far too much on methodologies, especially ways of quantifying environmental impacts, such as monetary evaluation. As we have seen in earlier chapters, EIA in general is essentially procedural and legislation for EIA and SEA should generally be about laying down minimum procedures which must be followed. We have already seen in Chapter 10 that the fact that there can be some differences in methodologies between EIA and SEA should make no difference to legislation which can, and it can be argued should, be consistent between project EIA and policy SEA. PAE also sees the policy formulation process as being highly fluid, which indeed it is, but that does not mean as is often argued that it is therefore difficult to identify where in the process formal EIA/SEA procedures should come. EIA/SEA is ideally suited for dealing with dynamic processes, not least because of its iterative nature, and in reality there are identifiable decision points in the policy formulation process, eg adoption of a plan or publication of a White Paper, which could be logically preceded by an SEA process.

Development plans

There could be considerable benefits from the application of SEA to local authority forward plans, such as Structure, Local and Unitary Development Plans in the UK. Applying SEA to plans should help resolve many of the environmental problems which become evident when an individual development project is examined. Formulating effective development plan policies should reduce the number of controversial and damaging applications later on in the planning process. It would also improve public discussion over environmental impacts by seeking to expose problems and difficulties before individual developments are even suggested. In the long term this should reduce public conflict over development and reduce the impact of development on the environment.

SEA at the forward planning level would enable the environmental implications of separate policies to be married, eg policies regarding office development and housing development, where the latter is often driven by the former, but housing provision often has greater impact on the environment. Furthermore, strategic environmental assessment would allow the most appropriate policy options to be chosen, for instance, with regard to housing provision. All options for new housing development should be examined, including new settlements, urban regeneration and peripheral expansion, and the least environmentally damaging mix of options chosen for a given area. Choices made at the development plan level would allow EIA at the project level to be more focused on the impacts on the local environment.

In February 1992 the UK Government published new planning guidance for the formulation of strategic development plans in the form of Planning Policy Guidance note 12 (PPG 12). This provides guidance to local authorities on the formulation of regional planning guidance, county-wide structure plans and district-wide local plans, and Unitary Development Plans (UDPs) in metropolitan areas. The Planning and Compensation Act 1991 established a new role for development plans as having a key role in helping to achieve environmentally sustainable development. Development plans can contribute to the objectives of sustainable development by providing a suitable framework for planning decisions.

The Town and Country Planning (Development Plan) Regulations 1991 (drawn up under the Planning and Compensation Act 1991) require for the first time local authorities to "have regard" to environmental considerations in preparing their general policies and proposals in structure plans and UDP Part Is. It states that

> "Most policies and proposals in all types of plan will have environmental implications, which should be appraised as part of the plan preparation process."

(para. 5.52 of PPG 12)

However, PPG 12 goes on in the same paragraph to say

"But the requirement to 'have regard' does not require a full environmental impact statement of the sort needed for projects likely to have serious environmental effects."

It is, of course, entirely appropriate for development plans to be subject to strategic environmental assessment, even though environmental protection is an inherent part of their purpose. This does not, however, mean that even a plan for which the environment is an integral part will not have significant damaging effects on the environment. Policies contained within a development plan while aiding environmental protection on the one hand may have adverse impacts on other aspects of the environment. Apart from which the policies contained in development plans address economic, social and environmental parameters. It is right therefore that all these policies are 'appraised' for their environmental impact. Preferably, the policies contained in development plans should be environmentally derived.

PPG 12 cites 'Policy Appraisal and the Environment' as the appropriate guidance which local authorities should follow in order to appraise their development plans. It suggests that the Guide (PAE) may help authorities to introduce a commonly accepted and systematic approach to the treatment of environmental issues in developing their planning policies. However, neither PPG 12 nor PAE provide any real guidance to local authorities as to how they are to go about appraisal of their development plans in practice. The Government had provided the requirement for the appraisal of development plans without any specific guidance as to how to do it; local authorities were effectively left to their own devices. This is very reminiscent of the lack of guidance provided by the Government with respect to project level EIA and the production of environmental statements; that guidance is still awaited, over five years after implementation. The Department of the Environment, however, employed consultants during 1993 to examine how local authorities were implementing the requirement of PPG 12 for policy appraisal of development plans and to provide draft guidance on best practice. That guidance was published in November 1993 (Environmental Appraisal of Development Plans: A Good Practice Guide) (UK DoE, 1993).

The development of appropriate methodologies for appraising development plans has been left to the initiative of individual local authorities. Not surprisingly only a few felt willing or able to get to grips with what the requirement of PPG 12 meant for them in practice. Two leading authorities have been Lancashire County Council and Kent County Council. Although the Government is intent on seeing appraisal as something different from strategic environmental assessment, both these authorities see what they are doing as a form of SEA. It has been their experience that has formed the basis for the best practice guidance produced by the consultants. The consultants approached the production of best practice guidance by identifying a series of sustainability criteria against which development plan policies can be evaluated (for example through the use of a matrix). These criteria comprise some fifteen sustainability criteria in three groups : global sustainability, natural resources, and local environmental quality. The fifteen criteria are:

> transport energy efficiency (trips); transport energy efficiency (modes); built environment energy efficiency; renew able energy potential; rate of CO_2 fixing; wildlife habitats;

> air quality; water conservation and quality; land and soil quality; minerals conservation;

> landscape and open land; urban environmental 'livability'; cultural heritage; open space; building quality.

At the end of the day, however much the Government may wish to distance itself from SEA proper, it is likely to be a form of strategic environmental assessment which emerges from the requirement in PPG 12 for environmental appraisal of policies, because that is the best way of incorporating environmentally sustainable objectives into plan formulation. Local authorities are recognising that their development plans need to be more objectives-led within an overall framework of contributing to environmentally sustainable development. This provides a suitable environment for the development of SEA.

In the Netherlands, a process of strategic environmental assessment already exists for land use plans, not dissimilar to that developing in the UK and as we have seen for the electricity supply industry.

Part IV
THE GLOBAL IMPERATIVE

Chapter 12

THE NEW AGE OF INTERNATIONAL AGREEMENT

Introduction

A number of events over recent years have signalled what might now be regarded as a new age of international agreement over the need for better environmental protection. Ozone depletion and global warming, in particular, present potentially such catastrophic implications for humanity and the rest of the planet that countries worldwide have been stirred into recognising that action needs to be taken now if the resources we are enjoying are likely to be available to future generations. That is the essence of 'sustainable development', put forward in the report - Our Common Future - of the World Commission on Environment and Development (the Brundtland Commission) in 1987 (WCED, 1987). The rising international concern culminated in the Earth Summit in Rio de Janeiro in June 1992 - the United Nations' Conference on Environment and Development (UNCED). The Earth Summit resulted in a number of agreements - by more than 170 countries - including a treaty on climate change, a biodiversity treaty, the Rio Declaration (a set of 27 principles on environmental and development issues), Agenda 21, a proposed UN Commission on sustainable development, a set of principles for conserving forests, and increases of around £1 billion per annum in Third World aid. Possibly the most significant document to be agreed at Rio, at least from the point of view of EIA, was Agenda 21, an 800-page plan, though not legally binding in the technical sense, for achieving sustainable development.

Agenda 21

Agenda 21 addresses the issues of environment and development in considerable detail covering Social and Economic

Dimensions (Section I), Conservation and management of resources for development (Section II), Strengthening the role of major groups (Section III), and Means of Implementation (Section IV). Most significant for EIA is Chapter 8 at the end of Section I: Integrating environment and development in decision-making. Three key features of this chapter stand out above all others. They are the recommendations:

·that environmental impact assessment 'should extend beyond the project level to policies and programmes';

·that governments should adopt a national strategy for sustainable development; and

·that enactment and enforcement of laws and regulations is essential for the implementation of most international agreements in the field of environment and development.

Paragraph 8.3 of Agenda 21 identifies the objectives of the first Programme Area covered by Chapter 8, that of integrating environment and development at the policy, planning and management levels:-

"The overall objective is to improve or restructure the decision-making process so that consideration of socio-economic and environmental issues is fully integrated and a broader range of public participation assured. Recognizing that countries will develop their own priorities in accordance with prevailing conditions, needs, national plans, policies and programmes, the following objectives are proposed:

(a) To conduct a national review of economic, sectoral and environmental policies, strategies and plans to ensure the progressive integration of environmental and developmental issues;

(b) To strengthen institutional structures to allow the full integration of environmental and developmental issues, at all levels of decision-making;

(c) To develop or improve mechanisms to facilitate the involvement of concerned individuals, groups and organisations in decision-making at all levels;

(d) To establish domestically determined procedures to integrate environment and development issues in decision-making."

Clearly EIA is one mechanism through which a number of these objectives can be met most effectively. However, the key paragraph supporting the need to develop and extend the principles of EIA is paragraph 8.5 (b):

"[the adoption of] comprehensive analytical procedures for prior and simultaneous assessment of the impacts of decisions, including the impacts within and among the economic, social and environmental spheres; these procedures should extend beyond the project level to policies and programmes; analysis should also include assessment of costs, benefits and risks;"

This paragraph makes an unequivocal connection between the application of EIA principles and sustainable development.

The UK published its National Sustainability Strategy on 25 January 1994 (Sustainable Development: the UK Strategy) (UK Government, 1994). It singularly failed to deliver the changes in decision making processes necessary to take the UK forward on a more sustainable path. While full of worthy sentiments, for example about reducing the need to travel, there was little in the way of new action beyond existing commitments and no evidence of a more objectives-led approach to policy formulation within which EIA and SEA were central. While the Prime

Minister announced the appointment of various advisory groups the evidence so far, eg the appointment of Green Ministers to each government department in the 1990 White Paper on the Environment (This Common Inheritance) (UK Government, 1990), suggests that such initiatives may be little more than window dressing. Without changes to decision making, eg a more environmentally sustainable transport policy rather than a series of largely unconnected initiatives (see motorway charging, Chapter 11) the objectives of sustainable development will remain largely beyond our grasp.

The strategy was seen as a huge disappointment by environmental groups and a genuine missed opportunity. On EIA there were no new commitments beyond those already made, for example those relating to the SACTRA recommendations (Chapter 5) on looking at the scope for SEA on road programmes, and the value of applying environmental appraisal (see Chapters 10 and 11) to all policies which affect the environment. (Even on these the evidence that much has happened since they were proposed more than two years ago is scant.) The strategy, unfortunately, failed to endorse the incorporation of EIA principles into all decision-making and to provide the mechanisms through which that can happen.

The European Community

At the end of 1992 the Council of the European Communities passed a resolution accepting the Fifth Action Programme on the Environment and Sustainable Development, also known as 'Towards Sustainability' (CEC, 1992; OJ, 1993). The Fifth Action Programme is seen as the Community's programme for implementing commitments made at the Earth Summit in Rio de Janeiro in June 1992.

The Fifth Action Programme includes a number of statements which reaffirm the Community's commitment to improving and extending the application of EIA. The preamble to the Council resolution includes:

> "[the Council] REAFFIRM the crucial importance of ensuring that environmental concerns are taken fully into account from the outset in the development of other policies and in the implementation of those policies, and the need for appropriate mechanisms within the Member States, the Council and the Commission to help achieve this integration, upon which the strategy advanced in the Programme relies;"

> "[the Council] INVITE the Commission to consider developing initiatives...including examination of the possibilities for the following areas....
>
> - the inclusion in new legislative proposals of a section dealing with the likely implications for the environment."

This latter point would mean an assessment of the likely significant environmental effects would have to be produced prior to the agreement of any new EC legislation. It would be even more encouraging if Member States would do likewise! The Programme also includes specific reference to EIA, including:

> "Given the goal of achieving sustainable development it seems only logical, if not essential, to apply an assessment of the environmental implications of all relevant policies, plans and programmes."

The Programme continues:

> "The integration of environmental assessment within the macro-planning process would not only enhance the protection of the environment and encourage optimisation of resource management but would also help to reduce those disparities in the international and inter-regional competition for new development projects which at present arise from disparities in assessment practices in the Member States."

"Finally, in pursuance of their commitment to integration of policies, the Commission and the Member States have already undertaken - at the Maastricht Summit - to take full account of environmental impact and the principle of sustainable development in the formulation and implementation of measures."

(page 66, Towards Sustainability)

Central to the Fifth Action Programme is the integration of all areas of policy. Page 76 of the Programme identifies practical reforms that will be undertaken including:

"-   in pursuance of the Treaty (Article 130r.2) and the objective of sustainable development, the environmental dimension will be fully incorporated into all other Community policies;

-     an assessment of the implications for the environment will be made in the course of drawing up Community policies and legislation with special care taken in the areas of internal market, international trade, industrial, energy, agriculture, transport, regional development and tourism;

-     Member States should undertake similar integration by applying environmental impact assessments to their own plans and programmes."

As implied above, the Community is also committed by the Action Programme to undertake EIAs in relation to regional development, and therefore in relation to its granting of aid to Member States. This has been an issue of great controversy over recent years, not least because the European Commission has failed to apply the principles of its own legislation effectively, ie the EIA Directive, when considering granting funds for regional development projects. One particular case has provided the focus for this controversy and contributed to amendments to the Regulations governing the allocation of Structural Funds. The case is that of the Burren, in Ireland and is addressed in some detail below.

Case study: The Burren

Concerns over the lack of environmental consideration in the allocation of the EC European Regional Development Fund came to the fore in Ireland when the Department of Finance of the Irish Government produced a National Development Plan covering Structural Fund spending for the period 1989-1993. An Taisce (Irish National Trust) became concerned at the marginal consideration being given to the environment. The National Plan was prepared with inadequate public participation and focused on large-scale infrastructure projects. Some of the most controversial schemes included tourism projects, such as leisure centres and golf courses which only became known about when planning applications were made. Among these tourism projects were Government-planned visitor centres in Ireland's National Parks. One in particular, that at Mullaghmore in the Burren, in the west of Ireland was to be located in a particularly sensitive area. The Government Office of Public Works announced its proposals early in 1991; the Burren had been newly designated as a National Park and site of international botanical importance. At the same time the Burren Action Group, supported by An Taisce and other environmental groups began campaigning locally, nationally and at EC level.

The focus of campaigning turned to the EC, requesting that funding be put on hold until an independent EIA had been undertaken. The issue was raised in the European Parliament and with European Commission officials who requested detailed documentation on the case. Pressure on the Irish Government led it to commission an EIA of the project and to undertake its own assessment. Both assessments, however, were heavily criticised by the environmental groups. In October 1992 the European Commission closed its file on the complaint thereby allowing the release of Structural Funds for the development, some 75% of the total cost. An Taisce and the World Wide Fund for Nature have since submitted a case to the European Court of Justice against the European Commission on the grounds that the decision to grant funding was in contravention of EC environmental policy (Case C-407/92, OJ C27, 30.1.1993). In Ireland, the Burren Action Group took the Irish Government to court, challenging its right to construct visitor centres and to proceed without planning permission. A Supreme Court decision found in favour of the environmentalists and granted an injunction stopping work on the site which had begun in late 1992 (ECAS, 1993). The Government subsequently ordered a formal public consultation. The Office of Public Works has now put forward amended proposals which would scale down the visitor centres proposed for Mullaghmore and other areas by about 12%. Planning applications will be submitted to the local authorities who are nevertheless expected to grant permission despite continuing opposition. Environmental groups are likely to appeal to the Irish planning appeals board - An Bord Pleanala - and subsequently to the courts. Scaling down the development hardly meets the concerns expressed about the overall environmental impact of the proposals on such a sensitive area.

Efforts to 'green' the Structural Funds go back to 1987, but the Burren case and the co-ordinated efforts of the various environmental groups involved provided the catalyst for securing change in the new Structural Fund framework and co-ordination Regulations (European Council Regulations EEC No. 2081/93 and 2082/93 respectively) covering the period 1994-1999, adopted after a Council Meeting on 19 July 1993. Other cases throughout the Community have also proved to be highly controversial, including a road tunnel in the Aspe Valley which threatens the last refuge for the brown bear in France, a hydro-electric dam project on the Aeheloos River in Greece, and a power station in the Canary Islands (now the subject of legal action by Greenpeace International against the European Commission). The revision of the Regulations illustrates the effect concerted effort by NGOs can have; more than 70 NGOs supported a memorandum setting out proposals for amending the Regulations which was press released throughout the EC in February 1992. That case was greatly helped by a highly critical report from the EC Court of Auditors in September 1992 on the integration of environmental concerns into the operation of the Structural Funds. Early in 1993 the Commission published proposals for revision of the regulations which incorporated many of the suggestions of NGOs.

The Structural Funds include the European Regional Development Fund (eg infrastructure developments), the European Social Fund (eg training) and the European Agricultural Guidance and Guarantee Fund (which includes agri-environmental and afforestation measures). The revised Regulations now require that development plans submitted under the regionally-specific objectives must contain an appraisal of the environmental situation in the region concerned and an evaluation of the environmental impact of the strategy and operations proposed, in terms of the principles of sustainable development. Such plans are also expected to mention the arrangements made to associate the competent environmental authorities at national, regional and local level which will be involved in the preparation and implementation of the projects envisaged under the plan and in ensuring compliance with the Community's environmental rules.

The effective implementation of these changes to the Regulations will be crucial as regional funding is increasingly directed towards major infrastructure linked to the Single Market, such as the Trans-European Network (TEN) and the Trans-European Road Network (TERN) in particular. Although many routes will be financed by Member States, in many cases they will also be part-financed through the Structural Funds. The revised Regulations mean that at least some form of strategic environmental assessment should be required for regional development plans where EC funding is concerned. Already, individual projects in receipt of EC funding should be subject to the existing EIA Directive (the Community is meant to comply with its own environmental legislation), but as we have seen this has had poor observance in practice. Furthermore, the failure of the EC to secure legislation for strategic environmental assessment more generally means that the designation of routes as part of TERN, for example, is not being complemented by strategic environmental assessment. The designation alone may have significant environmental effects, even if no new road building is proposed since it may result in attracting considerable amounts of traffic: after all, the TERN is supposed to identify suitable strategic routes for heavy goods vehicles across Europe.

The Espoo Convention on Trans-Boundary Impacts

The United Nations Economic Commission for Europe (UNECE) Convention on environmental impact assessment in a transboundary context was signed by 27 countries and the European Community at Espoo in Finland on 25 February 1991. Apart from applying to many more countries, the Convention elaborates considerably on the trans-boundary provisions of the EC Directive on EIA. Article 7 of the EC Directive requires that where a project is likely to have a significant effect on another Member State that Member State must be consulted and information provided to it in the same way as to the nationals of the Member State within which the project is to be located. The Espoo convention first of all requires EIA to be carried out prior to a decision to authorise or undertake a proposed activity (listed in Appendix I to the Convention) likely to cause a significant adverse transboundary impact. The convention also sets out general guidance for identifying criteria for determining significant adverse impacts (Appendix III to the Convention). Parties to the convention must provide for an opportunity for the public in the country affected to participate in the relevant EIA procedures which must be equivalent to that provided to the public in the country of origin. Perhaps most importantly, the Convention encourages parties to the Convention to carry out EIA for policies, plans and programmes, ie strategic environmental assessment:

> "Environmental impact assessments as required by this Convention shall, as a minimum requirement, be undertaken at the project level of the proposed activity. To the extent appropriate, the Parties shall endeavour to apply the principles of environmental impact assessment to policies, plans and programmes."
>
> (Article 2.7 of the Espoo Convention)

Unlike the EC Directive on EIA the Convention also makes provision for post-project monitoring (see Chapter 8).

The amendments to the EC Directive, eagerly awaited by many and expected during 1994, are likely to include proposals to incorporate fully the Espoo Convention into the Directive and so enable the EC to ratify the Convention.

United Nations Economic Commission for Europe (UNECE) Task Force

The UNECE established a task force, led by the United States of America, in 1990 to examine the application of environmental impact assessment principles to policies, plans and programmes. In its recommendations to member governments of the Economic Commission for Europe (UNECE, 1991) the task force recommended that EIA should be considered on a par with economic and social issues in the development of, and decisions on policies, plans and programmes and that EIA should be carried out where the possibility of significant environmental impact cannot reasonably be excluded. Encouragingly, the task force recognised that EIA for policies, plans and programmes should, as much as possible, reflect the principles of EIA applied to projects, even though it may differ somewhat, and that EIA at the policy, plan or programme level should not substitute for EIA at project level. It recognised that the goals of EIA remain the same, whether at project level or at policy, plan or programme level, ie to ensure that interested governmental and non-governmental parties are alerted at the earliest possible time to the potential environmental impacts and that those concerns are fully incorporate into decision making. The task force also encouraged the implementation of EIA through legislation and that any separate legislation, eg SEA legislation separate from that for project EIA or sectoral EIA legislation, should be linked to encourage integrated environmental management.

Both the Espoo Convention and the Task Force's recommendations point very clearly in the direction of establishing formal SEA procedures in member countries to facilitate sustainable development. However, given the 'soft' nature of these agreements it is perhaps not surprising that member countries have been rather slow to establish SEA procedures, certainly in legislation.

Developing countries

It is a commonly held misconception that there is little EIA experience in developing countries. In fact some developing countries have been carrying out EIAs for many years and some had established formal requirements and procedures before many western countries. Kenya is one example where EIA has been a cornerstone of the national development policy since the end of the 1970s but for which there is no comprehensive legislative base. EIA is included in rudimentary form in some sectoral legislation, but suffers from inconsistency in approach across sectors, the absence of clear legal guidelines and the use of often wide discretionary powers enabling environmental protection objectives to be overridden (Ogolla, 1992). Similarly, Malaysia has had EIA administrative procedures since 1979 and legally mandatory EIA for certain activities since 1985 through amendments to the Environmental Quality Act 1974. This was extended with the EIA Order 1987 (which came into effect in April 1988) subjecting 19 categories of activities to EIA. However, as so often found elsewhere, poor quality of EIA bedevils the system, including inadequate scoping, consideration of alternatives, prediction of magnitude of impacts and their significance and commitment to implementation of mitigation measures (Ibrahim, 1992).

While many developing countries have often had some form of project level EIA for some years the effectiveness of such procedures has left much to be desired often because of a lack of a legal basis for implementing and enforcing EIA requirements. Furthermore, the methodologies used for EIA in developed countries are not necessarily readily applicable or transferable to developing countries which may have very different social, cultural and institutional systems, lack of specialist expertise and different value systems, eg in terms of what constitutes 'significant' impacts on the environment (Biswas and Agarwala, 1992).

In many cases, of course, especially over recent years, the requirement for EIA in developing countries has frequently been at the insistence of aid agencies. Major aid agencies now have reasonably well established screening procedures and EIA requirements before granting aid to developing countries. However, as we have seen in the examples discussed in Chapter 6 in relation to public participation these systems have not proved to be fool-proof and major agencies such as the World Bank have ended up with egg on their face over environmentally damaging projects such as the Sardar Sarovar dam project in India. Often this is because of inadequate consideration of the impact of the project on local communities, especially the issue of resettlement, and the lack of public involvement. Government authorities and institutions in some developing countries also have a tendency to concentrate unduly on technical detail and not on the information most necessary for decision making.

In the UK, the Overseas Development Administration (ODA) which administers overseas aid has its own Manual of Environmental Appraisal (ODA, 1992) which provides guidance on integrating environmental considerations into decision making about aid allocation. The ODA's ten basic principles governing environmental appraisal include the requirement for all ODA officers to ensure that aid-funded policies, programmes and projects in which they are involved are environmentally acceptable, and that if environmental or social concerns are likely to be dealt with inadequately by a developing country or a project or programme is likely to have unacceptable environmental or social costs, the ODA should reject it. The manual provides guidance primarily for EIA in relation to the project cycle, although some of it is also of relevance to programmes and plans and there is specific reference to sectoral EIA. Inevitably, it has most often been the project stage at which aid agencies have traditionally become involved. The same is also true of the guidance followed by the European Commisson (based on good practice guidance produced by the OECD) in granting EC assistance to developing countries in Asia, Latin America and the Mediterranean. The Commission also provides assistance, through the Lomé IV Convention to countries in Africa, the Caribbean and the Pacific, and published its own Environmental Manual in 1993 which follows the arrangements established by the Convention to ensure a proper consideration of the environmental consequences of development projects and programmes.

The World Bank has established its own Operational Directive on EIA updated at regular intervals (OD 4.00, 1989; OD 4.01, 1991; OD 4.02, 1992). The guidance is elaborated on in the three volumes of its Environmental Assessment Sourcebook (World Bank, 1991). Although again largely focused on project cycle EIA the Sourcebook does encourage regional EIAs when a number of development activities are planned or proposed for a relatively localised geographical area, such as several projects in one watershed; and sectoral EIAs to examine cumulative impacts of multiple projects planned in the same sector. An example of the latter can be seen in an SEA carried out by the World Bank for a five-year Nigerian Government programme of road maintenance in Nigeria (Therivel et al, 1992). Increasingly, the World Bank is recognising the need to apply EIA at more strategic levels to augment, not replace, EIA at the project level (Goodland and Sadler, 1993). Essentially, the application of SEA to overseas development policies and programmes can be seen as a way of checking the consistency of such policies with the principles and guidelines of sustainable development developed by international agencies and through protocols, such as the agreements at the Earth Summit in Rio. Such assessments are no longer simply desirable, they are now crucial to meeting sustainable development objectives.

Arguably, the focus by aid agencies on requiring project-level EIA has meant that consideration of the environment has occured too late in the process to consider adequately the wider impacts of selecting a particular direction or programme for development. This is particularly apparent in the case of very large projects such as hydro-electric dams which are likely to have very significant impacts on the environment and affect a large number of people, but for which many of the alternatives have already been ruled out because of earlier decisions at the policy and plan levels. These are perhaps some of the best reasons why strategic environmental assessment is urgently required in developing countries so that major development plans and programmes, as opposed to simply projects, can be assessed for their environmental implications and alternative strategies considered. Arguably, establishing effective SEA should be a far greater priority for developing countries and for aid agencies than improving established project EIA procedures: it makes little sense to have good quality project EIA if the decision to build a major dam, for example, has effectively already been taken. Project EIA is then reduced to the identification of little more than marginal mitigation measures. With SEA in place a more environmentally sustainable route might have been identified in the first place.

Chapter 13

EIA AND POLLUTION CONTROL - THE CONVERGENCE OF PARALLEL LINES

Introduction

In recent years we have begun to see the previously demarcated processes of pollution control and EIA slowly coming together. Traditionally, pollution control has been activated through sectoral legislation controlling emissions to land, air and water separately. EIA has traditionally been associated with development control and land use planning and has variously been legislated for through sectoral legislation and/or framework legislation. Yet there has always been considerable overlap, for instance between the authorisation required for pollution control and authorisation giving consent to build a proposed project. But traditionally, development consent and pollution control authorisation have continued along parallel lines without ever being considered together. That process is beginning to change as a more integrated approach to pollution control is being considered and the overlaps with the EIA system become ever-more pronounced.

Integrated Pollution Control (IPC) as now exists in the UK and Integrated Pollution Prevention and Control (IPPC) as proposed in the EC addresses emissions to all media - land, air and water - through a single authorisation process and necessarily incorporates similar approaches to EIA prior to consent being given. For example, under the UK IPC system certain information on the likely environmental impact of the proposed emissions is required to be provided before IPC authorisation can be given so that Her Majesty's Inspectorate of Pollution (HMIP) is provided with the necessary information to come to a decision on whether to give authorisation or not. This information does not amount to a full EIA, but is an environmental assessment of those factors that are relevant to the processes concerned with the authorisation.

Clearly, for new factories or industrial plant which would be subject to IPC authorisation (ie those processes and/or substances prescribed as being subject to IPC) planning permission will also be required from the local planning authority or from the relevant Secretary of State, eg the Secretary of State for Trade and Industry where a power station is concerned (where deemed planning consent is required in addition to licensing as an electricity generator). In such a situation, a simplified form of assessment will be produced for IPC authorisation and an EIA would be carried out for planning consent and an ES produced. In most cases, pollution data and information would be provided for the ES, and this would be, or could be, the same as the assessment for IPC. It makes considerable sense for the ES to satisfy the requirements for both the IPC authorisation and for the EIA requirements. Both authorisation processes would therefore need to occur more or less together as should be so in any case. One process should not be pre-empted by another, eg IPC authorisation should not be influenced by whether or not the plant has already been given planning consent, or vice versa. The proposed EC Directive on IPPC (see below) makes provision in Article 5 (2) for information supplied in accordance with the EIA Directive to be included in an IPPC application where it fulfils the requirements of Article 5.

Integrated pollution control

Integrated Pollution Control (IPC) was established in the UK by Part 1 of the Environmental Protection Act 1990. It created for the first time a single system of pollution control (for emissions to all media: air, water and land) for major industrial processes ('prescribed processes'). A separate regime for controlling emissions to air alone was also established under Part 1 of the act, for which local authorities are the enforcing authorities.

IPC requires operators to apply for prior authorisation from Her Majesty's Inspectorate of Pollution (HMIP) to operate the process. The operator must advertise the fact that an application has been made and details of the application must be placed on the public register. In granting authorisations HMIP has a duty to include conditions which ensure:

> ·that the operator will use the best available techniques not entailing excessive cost (BATNEEC) to prevent, or else minimise, the release of certain substances (prescribed in regulations) into any environmental medium (air, land or water);

> ·that any substances that are released, or which might cause harm if released into any environmental medium, are rendered harmless;

> ·that where a process is likely to involve releases to more than one medium, BATNEEC is used to minimise pollution to the environment as a whole having regard to the best practicable environmental option (BPEO) as regards the substances that may be released; and

> ·compliance with any direction given by the Secretary of State for the Environment to implement European Community or international obligations or any other statutory requirements.

IPC came into force for new or modified processes in April 1991. All other existing processes will come under IPC control at the latest by 1996 in accordance with a phased programme laid down in regulations. Applications for the first phase, including most large combustion plants, had to be made by 30 April 1991.

The key regulations relating to Part 1 of the Act are:

The Environmental Protection (Prescribed Processes and Substances) Regulations 1991 (SI 472) and as amended by SI 1991 No. 836, SI 1992 No. 614, SI 1993 No. 1749 and SI 1993 No. 2405 (and under review in 1994)

The Environmental Protection (Applications, Appeals and Registers) Regulations 1991 (SI 507)

The Environmental Protection (Authorisation of Processes) (Determination Periods) Order (No. 513) 1991.

The Department of the Environment and the Welsh Office also published a guide 'Integrated Pollution Control: A Practical Guide' (October 1990) (UK DoE, 1990).

Applicants for IPC authorisation must provide an assessment of the environmental consequences of any emissions relating to the process being considered for authorisation. The Environmental Protection (Applications, Appeals and Registers) Regulations 1991 stress that this assessment does not amount to a detailed environmental impact assessment, but that it should be an assessment of the main areas where the process is likely to impact on the environment (whether globally, regionally or locally) and, against that, a justification of the process/technique to be used (Regulation 2 (g) and (i)). This requirement was secured as a result of lobbying by conservationists during the passage of the Environmental Protection Bill (CPRE, 1990).

Although the Environmental Protection Act represents something of a landmark in industrial regulation there have been a number of difficulties with implementation. From the beginning HMIP has been dogged by lack of resources which has inevitably meant that enforcement, for example of the regulations requiring operators to provide information on the environmental consequences of their processes (a simplified form of environmental impact assessment), has been poor. Staff allocation as of 1 April 1992 was 365, but at that time there were only 280 people in post. Even this allocation was well short of the 434 staff HMIP estimated was needed (WWF, 1992). A review of implementation of Part 1 of the Environmental Protection Act 1990 was carried out by Earth Resources Research for the World Wide Fund for Nature (WWF, 1992). It identified a number of problems with implementation including a lack of transparency in HMIP decision making, poor quality of applications and assessments, inadequate monitoring, difficulties with public access to information especially due to commercial confidentiality (information can be withheld from public registers on these grounds), and poor enforcement through prosecution resulting in inadequate deterrence.

Planning and Pollution

The closer integration of planning and pollution control is beginning to happen, and not just in relation to IPC. In June 1992 the UK Government published a draft Planning Policy Guidance note (PPG) on Planning and Pollution Controls. Its intention is to give guidance to local authorities for the first time on the relevance of pollution controls to the exercise of planning functions. It is also intended to provide guidance on the relationship between authorities' planning responsibilities and the separate statutory responsibilities exercised by local authorities and other pollution control bodies, principally under the Environmental Protection Act 1990 and the Water Resources Act 1991.

The draft PPG recognises that the possibility of a new development causing pollution or waste is one aspect of the overall environmental effect of that development or the use of land, and that it may therefore be a material consideration to be taken into account in deciding whether to grant planning permission. However, the draft PPG stresses that it is not the job of planning authorities to duplicate or substitute the controls which are the responsibility of other agencies. The draft PPG includes advice on the role of development plans and Regional Planning Guidance in establishing a framework for environmental protection including policies on pollution and waste. It is, though, at the point of development control where there has traditionally been least integration between the two processes. The draft PPG advises that where a development proposal seems likely to raise significant pollution issues, planning authorities should seek advice from pollution control authorities on whether the development is likely to meet pollution control objectives.

Annex 7 of the draft PPG provides guidance on Environmental Assessment, in particular in relation to projects falling under the Town and Country Planning (Assessment of Environmental Effects) Regulations 1988 and pollution control considerations. The guidance recognises that an environmental statement prepared under the regulations provides an important opportunity for the local planning authority to obtain information on the pollution aspects of the proposed development and the implications these may have for the development and use of land. The regulations allow for statutory consultees, including pollution control agencies, to be consulted and to make representations to the planning authority. However, the guidance does not go so far as to advise, as suggested above, that where a development requires both planning consent and pollution control authorisation a joint environmental statement should be produced. Interestingly, the more significant reference to EIA in the draft PPG is not in Annex 7, but in the section on development control. Under a sub-heading 'Need and Alternative Sites' the guidance states explicitly for the first time in Government guidance or regulations (para 3.11) that:

> "Applicants do not normally have to prove the need for their proposed development, or discuss the merits of alternative sites, except in the case of an application which must be accompanied by an environmental statement (see paragraph 3.12 below); this applies equally to development which will generate pollution or waste or which is designed to treat or dispose of waste. However, the nature of such developments may make the need for the development and the lack of availability of suitable alternative sites material to the planning decision."

Paragraph 3.12 goes on to say that in cases which would not have significant environmental effects, applicants should not have to provide detailed supporting evidence to establish need for the development, or the advantages of the preferred site over alternatives. Where environmental statements are provided, however, "they may - and as a matter of practice normally should - include an outline discussion of the main alternatives studied by the developer and an indication of the reasons for choosing the development proposed, taking account of environmental effects." This is a somewhat stronger form of words than that found in Schedule 3 of the EIA Regulations which leaves the provision of information on alternatives initially to the discretion of the developer (see Chapter 5).

The publication of the PPG on Planning and Pollution Controls in its final form is still awaited.

Integrated pollution prevention and control (IPPC)

On 14 September 1993 the European Commission adopted a proposal (COM (93) 423) for a framework Directive on the integrated prevention and control of pollution from industrial plants which has a major environmental impact. It is anticipated that IPPC will replace the sectoral approach taken to date, eg the Air Framework Directive (84/360/EEC) would be repealed. Industrial plants with a serious environmental impact (as defined in Annex I to the Directive) would be required to obtain a permit before starting operation. Existing plants would be required to obtain a permit by 30 June 2005 at the latest. Permits would be granted in a similar way to the UK's IPC process. They would have to be renewed every ten years and renewal would have to take account of developments in best available techniques (BAT).

The proposed Directive would allow Member States to lay down their own emission limits values, following the principle of subsidiarity. The public is to be given access to information relating to authorisations and the public will have the right to comment on applications. Operating licences will normally have to be granted within six months of application by one authority given overall responsibility by the Member State (a one-stop shop).

In many ways this EC proposal is based on IPC in the UK and the UK Government has been instrumental in the development of the draft Directive. However, perhaps the most striking difference is the focus of IPPC on BAT rather than BATNEEC. In practice this difference may not be so great depending on the final definition given to BAT in the Directive. It is currently defined as those techniques which are "industrially feasible, in the relevant sector, from a technical and economic point of view" although it also requires that account be taken of costs and benefits to the environment. It is likely that such a definition would be required for the UK at least to agree the Directive, so that it did not contradict IPC.

The Commission hopes that the draft Directive would be adopted by the Council in 1994 with transposition on 30 June 1995. This may be over-optimistic. The legal basis for the Directive is Article 130s as the main objective is to improve environmental protection. The draft Directive includes provision for an advisory committee to the Commission to advise on future changes to the annex lists of industries concerned and of principle polluting substances.

Case study: Implementing the Large Combustion Plants Directive

A good example of how the environmental impact assessment process is applied at too late a stage in the decision-making process, and how the connections between pollution control and EIA are not yet being made, is to be found with Flue Gas Desulphurisation (FGD). An SEA is clearly needed on the whole national plan for the reduction of air emissions (drawn up under Integrated Pollution Control as part of the Environmental Protection Act 1990 to comply with the EC Large Combustion Plants Directive, 88/609/EEC) in order to identify first the role of FGD in an SO_2 reduction strategy, and second, the most appropriate choice of technologies or processes for a particular FGD site. The project EIA could then be more focused on the environmental impacts associated with that particular FGD installation. A proposal to require just such an assessment of the national plan was rejected by the UK Government during the passage of the Environmental Protection Bill 1990 (CPRE, 1990). The Minister, in replying to the amendment said:

> "...we are not convinced that formal detailed assessments have the same part to play in strategic level discussions such as those involved in making plans for national emission reductions."

(Lord Reay, Hansard 19.6.90, col 857)

The two main FGD processes available for reducing sulphur dioxide (SO_2) emissions from coal-fired power stations have quite different impacts on the environment. The limestone-gypsum process is generally more environmentally damaging than the regenerative process, such as Wellman-Lord. The former requires large quantities of extracted limestone which might come not only from National Parks, but also from other important landscape areas, including Areas of Outstanding Natural Beauty and many non-designated areas.

However, the problem is much wider than just the issue of extraction. The consequential impacts of extraction, particularly involving transport of materials, whether by road or rail, could have very significant impacts in the particular areas concerned, often, for instance, where roads are already congested. In addition, the disposal of waste gypsum - and there will always be contaminated waste gypsum to be disposed of, even if a proportion of clean gypsum can be used in wall board manufacture - will have transport impacts and wider environmental impacts resulting from the need for land-fill and the possible leaching of contaminants. The swamping of the gypsum market could also have long-term impacts on the viability of the limestone-gypsum FGD process. Similar arguments could be employed in relation to sulphuric acid and sulphur compounds produced as by-products of the regenerative process, though it uses comparatively small quantities of sodium sulphite solution as raw material.

Unfortunately, there is no evidence to suggest that the relative environmental impacts of the alternative FGD processes have yet been taken into account in the UK. Environmental statements produced by one of the electricity generators, Power Gen, for instance, for proposed FGD plants at the coal-fired stations of Ferrybridge and Ratcliffe-on-Soar, make no mention of the alternative regenerative process. Regenerative processes have not even been considered, let alone dismissed. The limestone-gypsum process has been chosen without wider environmental considerations in mind.

A proper EIA, even at the project level, should include a full assessment of alternatives, with the final choice of process being made as a result of the EIA process. But even so, such an EIA could have no bearing on the choice of technologies for other FGD installations or, indeed, the overall role of FGD within an SO_2 reduction strategy. Neither would it be able to take adequate account of the impact that a particular FGD installation might have on the relevant by-product markets; that requires adequate information to be available about decisions being made regarding all other FGD installations.

This highlights the problem only too well: that an environmental impact assessment at the project level alone is actually inadequate. The EIAs that have been carried out for existing FGD proposals to date have, to compound matters further, been far from adequate in their own right.

One of the central objectives in setting conditions of authorisation under IPC in Part I of the Environmental Protection Act 1990 is to have regard to the best practicable environmental option when ensuring that the best available techniques not entailing excessive cost (BATNEEC) are used for minimising pollution. If an SEA was carried out on the national air emissions reduction plan it is likely to result in a mixed-method approach to reducing sulphur dioxide emissions, using not only FGD processes, but also fuel switching and energy conservation and efficiency. SEA would enable the Best Practicable Environmental Options (BPEOs), or mix of options, to be identified which would be implemented at the project level through the application of BATNEEC by HMIP.

At one end of the scale an SEA on the national plan would address the various options for sources of energy, including the use of gas, low-sulphur coal, renewables, 'clean coal' technologies, combined heat and power and the role of energy conservation and efficiency for achieving the targets set out in the national plan. Energy efficiency and the fitting of scrubbing technology may be particularly appropriate for the range of industrial installations, such as oil refineries; for the Electricity Supply Industry (ESI) there are perhaps many more options which should be addressed, including energy conservation, FGD in its various guises and fuel switching. At the other end of the scale, and having established the broad environmental parameters and options, the SEA on the national plan would address more specific aspects of particular sectors of industry, such as the various ways of achieving FGD in the ESI or the range of options open to oil refineries.

Chapter 14

BACK TO THE FUTURE

We have seen in the preceding chapters how EIA has developed over the last quarter of a century. Project EIA is now well established throughout many parts of the world, although its effectiveness is not infrequently hampered by poor enforcement and the lack of more strategic EIA to provide a suitable context within which it can operate.

Some countries, China for instance, are struggling to come to terms with public participation in the EIA process, fundamental as it is to effective and worthwhile EIA. But we should not take it for granted that public participation is always provided for adequately in developed countries. In many cases there is considerable scope for improvement. Even if it occurs there may be questions as to whether it occurs early enough or is seen by decision makers as anything more than a token gesture.

Increasingly EIA is helping to integrate decision making where traditionally it has been unconnected, in particular land use planning and pollution control. The development of integrated (multi-media) approaches to pollution control at the project level by its very nature involves elements of EIA. But at the plan and programme level, where a strategy for pollution abatement and/or prevention is set out, EIA/SEA has an even more crucial role to play in helping to determine the best environmental options or mix of options.

The issue of alternatives and choice of options should be central to effective EIA, but all too often is missing in its application. This is particularly true where EIA is bolted on to existing decision making processes instead of being properly incorporated into that decision making at the earliest possible stage. When we look at the environmental problems facing developing countries embarking on ambitious development programmes we can recognise all too clearly the hallmark of project EIA applied too late to influence the real decisions.

Central to EIA is the provision of information to a wide audience of interested bodies and individuals. The earlier EIA occurs in the decision making process the more effective will be their participation. We have seen how international agreements, such as Agenda 21, are encouraging nations to pursue paths towards sustainable development through, inter alia, the application of EIA to all levels of decision making. This is not just so that the environment is included, but also so that the people concerned are given opportunities to participate in the decisions that affect them.

The agreements signed at Rio in 1992 brought a degree of optimism to many environmentalists that perhaps governments were willing at last to bite the bullet and take some real and signficant action to combat the environmental threats hanging over the world. The evidence so far that anything has changed is not terribly encouraging: the UK Government's National Sustainabiltiy Strategy, for instance, was a grave disappointment. The rhetoric of sustainability emanating from the UK Government, which includes many fine sentiments, sits very ill at ease alongside its (apparently) greater desire to deregulate and to play the subsidiarity card whenever new regulation is suggested from Brussels. We have heard fine words before - on the use of financial instruments - but apart from the decision to raise excise duty on petrol by 5% per year most such initiatives, (eg motorway charging, VAT on fuel) have been to raise cash rather than manage demand. We have seen precious little real action in the environmental sphere even though such instruments could have an important role to play alongside regulation.

On the other hand, the deregulation initiative has every likelihood of throwing a number of babies out with the bathwater. If environmental regulation, such as EIA requirements, really do impose such huge burdens on industry, the logical extension of the deregulation argument is to have no regulation at all and remove all regulatory burdens from industry. Do that and you end up with the environment of Eastern Europe. Industry accepts - it has no choice - regulation and control imposed by society which in turn imposes costs on both industry and society alike. But it also encourages industry to be efficient, to minimise its inputs of raw materials, energy and water while minimising its environmentally harmful outputs. The jobs versus environment argument, which all too often rears its ugly head, simply will not wash. Notwithstanding the fact that environmental protection often creates jobs, the argument that environmental regulation reduces the competitiveness of British industry compared with that of, say, developing countries and the Pacific rim is anything but conclusive. Strong environmental regulation has not hindered the competitiveness of Japan and Germany, it has encouraged efficiency and created jobs in new industries. Industry in the West is already highly mechanised and automated and highly efficient by comparison with much of industry in developing countries. That should create competitive advantage not disadvantage. And surely the West owes it to itself as well as developing countries to take the first steps on the road to sustainable development. If we can't how can we expect them to do so.

EIA has moved on from its earliest days. It is no longer just about reconciling the environment with economic growth (achieving a balance). The context for decision making is now that of sustainable development which places the environment centre stage. While EIA continues to present information to decision makers, those same decision makers can no longer simply ignore that information. Sustainable development implies that if economic development would unduly compromise the environment, the environment should win through.

Debates over environmental, social and economic sustainabilty do not mean that one necessarily has to be compromised over the others. EIA provides a mechanism for identifying ways forward which maximise sustainability for all three factors, allowing decision makers to choose the options that are most sustainable. There is, however, an environmental and social imperative behind the concept of sustainable development. That was the purpose of the Rio Earth Summit, to find ways of protecting the Earth from the predicted ravages of economic development. We should not forget that it is the consequences of unbridled development that have brought us to this new age of international agreement on environmental protection.

It is, then, the concept of sustainable development that now provides the best opportunity for EIA to make its real impact on decision making. Whether it will depends crucially on whether governments are willing and ready to make the most of that opportunity. EIA in turn offers probably the best mechanism for incorporating sustainability into decision making.

REFERENCES

Alder, J (1993), Environmental Impact Assessment - The Inadequacies of English Law, Journal of Environmental Law, Vol. 5, No. 2, pp 203-220.

ANZECC (Australian and New Zealand Environment and Conservation Council) (1991), A National Approach to Environmental Impact Assessment in Australia, October 1991 (reprinted in June 1992)

Bass, R (1990), California's Experience with Programmatic Environmental Impact Reports, Project Appraisal, Vol 5, Number 4, December 1990.

Batelle Institute (1978), Rapport final de l'étude selection des projects destines à etre soumis à une évaluation d'impact sur l'environnement, CEC, ENV/513/78, French translation, Brussels, July 1978.

Binnie and Partners (1991a), Water for the Future in Kent: Scope of Environmental Assessment, January 1991.

Binnie and Partners (1991b), Water for the Future in Kent: Issues and Options, July 1991.

Biswas, A K and Agarwala, S B C (eds.) (1992), Environmental Impact Assessment for Developing Countries, Butterworth-Heinemann, Oxford, UK.

Carson, R L (1968), Silent Spring, Houghton Mifflin, Boston.

Central Electricity Generating Board (CEGB) (1988) Evidence to the Hinkley C Public Inquiry

Cerny, R J and Sheate, W R (1992), Strategic Environmental Assessment in the European Community: Amending the EA Directive, Environmental Policy and Law, Vol. 22, No. 3, pp 154 - 159, June 1992.

Coles, T, Fuller, K and Slater, M (1992), Practical Experience of Environmental Assessment in the UK, paper to IEA Conference: Advances in Environmental Assessment, 29th October 1992.

Commission of the European Communities (CEC) (1972), 'Declaration Finale' of the Heads of State of Government, Bulletin of the European Communities, October 1972, 10, point 8.

Commission of the European Communities (CEC) (1979), 13th General Report on the Activities of the European Communities.

Commission of the European Communities (1992), Fifth Action

Programme on the Environment: Towards Sustainability, A European Community Programme of Policy and Action in relation to the Environment and Sustainable Development, 1992.

Commission of the European Communities (1993), Report from the Commission of the Implementation of Directive 85/337/EEC, COM (93) 28 final - Vol 12, Brussels, 2 April 1993.

CPRE (Council for the Protection of Rural England) (1990) Briefing to the House of Commons Second Reading of the Environmental Protection Bill, 9.1.90 (and subsequent briefings to both Houses of Parliament).

CPRE (1991a), Environmental Assessment and Private Bill Procedure, April 1991.

CPRE (1991b), The Environmental Assessment Directive - Five Years On, CPRE, May 1991.

CPRE (1991c) Letter of Complaint to the European Commission regarding Wilton Power Station, Teesside, 15 April 1991.

CPRE (1991d) Complaint to the European Commission regarding the UK implementation of environmental assessment for roads, 6 September 1991.

CPRE (1992), 'Mock' EC Directive on Environmental Assessment: Proposals for amending EC Directive 85/337/EEC, August 1992.

CPRE (1993) Letter to Tim Eggar, Minister for Energy, from CPRE, 22.2.93.

Deansley, C, Papanicolaou, C and Turner, A (1993), Badlands: Essential Environmental Law for Property Professionals, Cameron May, London.

Department of Transport (1992) Assessing the Environmental Impact of Road Schemes, Standing Advisory Committee on Trunk Road Assessment (SACTRA) Report, 1992, London: HMSO.

Department of Transport (1993) Paying for Better Motorways: A consultation paper, Cm 2200, May 1993, London: HMSO.

van Eck, M (1993), EIA for Policy, Plans and Programmes in the Netherlands, paper to IAIA 13th Annual Meeting, Shanghai, China, June 1993.

ENDS (1993), Taking Stock of Environmental Assessment, ENDS

Report No. 221, pp 20-24.

Ehrlich, P R and Ehrlich A H (1972), Population, Resources, Environment: Issues in Human Ecology, Freeman and Co., San Francisco.

Euro Citizen Action Service (ECAS) (1993), EC Environment Policy and the Role of the Citizen, Report of a conference held on 23-24 November 1993.

Fearnside, P M (1993), The Canadian Feasibility Study of the Three Gorges Dam Proposed for China's Yangtze River: The Impact Assessment Profession's Dirtiest Laundry, paper given to IAIA 13th Annual Meeting, Shanghai, China, June 1993.

Gardiner, J (1992), Strategic environmental assessment and the water environment, Project Appraisal, Vol. 7, No. 3, pp 165-169.

Geddes, A (1992), Locus Standi and EEC Environmental Measures, Journal of Environmental Law, Vol.4, No. 1, pp 29-39.

Goodland, R and Sadler, B (1993), Strategic Environmental Assessment for Sustainable Development, paper to IAIA 13th Annual Meeting, Shanghai, China, June 1993.

Gorman, T (1993), MWD Builds Reservoir of Goodwill, Los Angeles Times, 12 April 1993.

Hardin, G (1968), The Tragedy of the Commons, Science, Vol. 162, pp 1243-1248.

Hunt, C D (1990), A Note on Environmental Impact Assessment in Canada, 20 Environmental Law 789.

Che Ibrahim, A K (1992) EIA experience in Malaysia, EIA Newsletter 7, Manchester.

Jacobs, F and Shanks, M (1986), Joint advice to CPRE re: Water Authority Privatisation, 7 October 1986.

Jones, C and Lee, N (1993), Post-auditing in Environmental Impact Assessment: the Greater Manchester Metrolink Scheme, Occassional Paper 37, 49 pp, Manchester EIA Centre.

Kramer, L (1991), The Implementation of Community Environmental Directives within Member States: Some Implications of the Direct Effect Doctrine, Journal of Environmental Law, Vol. 3, No. 1, pp 39-56.

Lee, N and Lewis, M D (1991), Environmental Assessment Guide for

Passenger Transport Schemes, prepared on behalf of the Passenger Transport Executive Group, Manchester.

Lee, N and Wood, C (1976), The Introduction of Environmental Impact Statements in the European Communities, CEC, ENV/197/76, May 1976.

Lee, N and Wood, C (1977), Methods of Environmental Impact Assessment for Major Projects and Physical Plans, CEC, ENV/36/78, December 1977; and Lee, N and Wood, C (1977), Environmental Impact Assessment of Physical Plans in the European Communities, CEC, ENV/37/78, December 1977.

Lee, N and Wood, C (1979), Environmental Impact Assessment and the Preparation of Economic Plans and Programmes in the European Communities, CEC, ENV/740/79, November 1979.

Lee, N and Wood, C (1984), Environmental Impact Assessment Procedures Within the European Community, in Roberts, R and Roberts, T (eds.), Planning and Ecology, Chapman and Hall, London, 1984.

Lewis, M D (1990), A tiered system of environmental impact assessment in Metropolitan (Greater Manchester) and Shire County (Cheshire) transport provision, Unpublished MSc thesis, University of Manchester, Manchester.

Macrory, R B (1992a), Environmental Assessment and EC Law: Case Law Analysis of Twyford Parish Council v Secretary of State for the Environment and Secretary of State for Transport; In the petition of the Kincardine and Deeside District Council, Journal of Environmental Law, Vol. 4, No. 2, pp 298-304.

Macrory, R B (1992b) Campaigners' Guide to Using EC Environmental Law, CPRE, June 1992.

McHarg, I (1969), Design With Nature, Natural History Press, New York.

Meadows, D H, Meadows, D L, Randers, J, and Behrens, W W, (1972), The Limits to Growth, A Report for the Club of Rome's Project on the Predicament of Mankind, London: Earth Island Limited, 1972.

Mitchell, B (1975), the Environmental Impact Statement: report of a seminar held in Louvain, Belgium, 12th December 1975, EEB/ECEL.

von Moltke, K (1977), The Legal Basis for Environmental Policy,

Environmental Policy and Law, Vol. 3, pp 136-140.

Morgan, R (1993), An Evaluation of Progress with Implementing the Environmental Assessment Requirements of the [New Zealand] Resource Management Act, paper to IAIA 13th Annual Meeting, Shanghai, China, June 1993 (and personal communication).

Official Journal of the European Communities (1973), First Programme of Action on the Environment, OJ No. C 112, Vol. 16, 20.12.73.

Official Journal of the European Communities (1977), Second Programme of Action on the Environment, OJ No. C 134, Vol. 20, 13.6.77.

Official Journal of the European Communities (1980), Proposal for a Council Directive concerning the assessment of the environmental effects of certain public and private projects, OJ No. C 169, 9.7.80 (CEC document: COM (80) 313 final).

Official Journal of the European Communities (1993) Fifth Action Programme on the Environment: Towards Sustainability, OJ No. C 138, Vol.1, 1993.

Ogolla, B D (1992), Environmental Management Policy and Law in Kenya, Environmental Policy and Law, Vol 22/23, pp 164 - 174.

O'Riordan, T and Turner, R K (1983), An Annotated Reader in Environmental Planning and Management, Urban and Regional Planning Series, Volume 30, Pergamon Press, Oxford.

Overseas Development Administration (ODA) (1992), Manual of Environmental Appraisal.

Probe International/Earthscan (1993), Damming the Three Gorges: What Dam Builders Don't Want You to Know (2nd edition).

Roberts, J, Cleary, J, Hamilton K, and Hanna, J (eds.) (1992), Travel Sickness: the Need for a Sustainable Transport Policy for Britain, Lawrence and Wishart, London.

Scannell, Y (1990), Environmental Assessment: Case Law Analysis of Michael Brown v An Bord Pleanala; Lewin and Rowley v Secretary of State for the Environment and Secretary of State for Transport, Journal of Environmental Law, Vol. 2, No. 2, pp 220-223.

Schrecker, T (1991), The Canadian Environmental Assessment Act: Tremulous Step Forward or Retreat into Smoke and Mirrors? Canadian

Environmental Law Reporter, Vol 5, p 192.

Selmi, D P (1984), "The Judicial Development of the California Environmental Quality Act," 18 U.C. Davis L. Rev. 197.

Sheate, W R (1984), The EEC Draft Directive on the Environmental Assessment of Projects: Its History, Development and Implications, Unpublished MSc thesis, University of London, Imperial College, September 1984.

Sheate, W R (1991), Public Participation: the Key to Effective Environmental Assessment, Environmental Policy and Law, Vol. 21, nos 3 & 4, pp 156 - 160, July 1991.

Sheate, W R (1992a) Lobbying for Effective Environmental Assessment, Long Range Planning, Vol. 25, No. 4, pp 90-98, August 1992.

Sheate, W R (1992b) Evidence to the North Yorkshire Power Lines Inquiry on behalf of CPRE, May 1992.

Sheate, W R (1992c), Strategic Environmental Assessment in the Transport Sector, Project Appraisal, Vol. 7, no. 3, pp 170 - 174, September.

Sheate, W R and Cerny, R J (1993), Legislating for EIA: Learning the Lessons, paper to IAIA 13th Annual Meeting, Shanghai, China, June 1993.

Sheate, W R and Macrory, R B (1989), Agriculture and the EC Environmental Assessment Directive: Lessons for Community Policy-Making, Journal of Common Market Studies, Vol. XXVIII, No. 1, pp 68-81.

Sippe, R and Ashe, J (1993), The New National Focus for Environmental Impact Assessment in Australia, paper to IAIA 13th Annual Meeting, Shanghai, China, June 1993.

Stuffman, C (1979), Minutes of evidence taken before the European Communities Committee (UK House of Lords, Sub-Committee G, Environment), 23.1.79, evidence heard in private.

Taylor, A (1990), A tiered system of EIA for the transport sector with specific reference to London, Unpublished MSc thesis, University of Manchester, Manchester.

TEST (1992), An Environmental Approach to Transport and Planning in Cardiff, report produced by Transport and Environment Studies (TEST) in association with Chris Isaac, commissioned by Cardiff Friends of the Earth.

Therivel, R, Wilson, E, Thompson, S, Heaney, D and Pritchard, D (1992), Strategic Environmental Assessment, Earthscan, London.

Trippier, D (1992), Letter of 5 August 1991 from the Minister for the Countryside to Fiona Reynolds, CPRE.

UK Department of the Environment (1989) Environmental Assessment: A Guide to the Procedures, London: HMSO.

UK Department of the Environment (1990), Integrated Pollution Control: A Practical Guide.

UK Department of the Environment (1991a), Policy Appraisal and the Environment: A guide for government departments, London: HMSO.

UK Department of the Environment (1991b), Monitoring Environmental Assessment and Planning, report by Wood, C and Jones, C, Manchester EIA Centre for DoE, London: HMSO.

UK Department of the Environment (1992), Letter to CPRE North Wilts, 30 June 1992.

UK Department of the Environment (1993), Environmental Appraisal of Development Plans: A Good Practice Guide, November 1993, London: HMSO.

UK Government (1990), This Common Inheritance, White Paper on the Environment, Cm 1200, London: HMSO.

UK Government (1994) Sustainable Development: the UK Strategy, Cm2426, January 1994, London: HMSO.

UK House of Lords (1981), Select Committee on the European Communities (Sub-Committee G, Environment), Environmental Assessment of Projects, 11th Report, Session 1980-81, with minutes of evidence, 3rd February, London: HMSO.

United Nations Conference on Environment and Development (UNCED) (1992), Agenda 21.

United Nations Economic Commission for Europe (UNECE) (1991), Policies and Systems of Environmental Impact Assessment, ECE/ENVWA/15, UN, New York; and Application of Environmental Impact Assessment Principles to Policies, Plans and Programmes, ECE/

ENVWA/WG.3/R.3, October 1991.

Waldegrave, W (1983), Supplementary explanatory memorandum on European Community legislation, from the Parliamentary Under Secretary of State, 2nd November 1983.

Wandesforde-Smith, G (1978), Environmental Impact Assessment in the European Community, Pre-print to publication (in 1979) in Zeitschrift für Umweltpolitik, 1978.

Webb, J. W and Sigal, L L (1992), Strategic Environmental Assessment in the United States, Project Appraisal, Vol. VII, No. 3, September, 1992).

Ward, A (1993), The Right to an Effective Remedy in European Community Law and Environmental Protection: A Case Study of United Kingdom Judicial Decisions Concerning the Environmental Assessment Directive, Journal of Environmental Law, Vol. 5, No. 2, pp 221-244.

Williams, R (1991), Direct Effect of EC Directive on Impact Assessment, Cambridge Law Journal, pp 382-384.

Woolf, Sir Harry (1992), Are the Judiciary Environmentally Myopic?, Journal of Environmental Law, Vol. 4, No. 1, pp 1-14.

World Bank (1991) Environmental Assessment Sourcebook, 3 Volumes, World Bank, Washington, D.C.

World Commission on Environment and Development (1987), Our Common Future, Oxford University Press, Oxford.

World Wide Fund for Nature (UK) (WWF) (1992), A Review of Part 1 of the Environmental Protection Act - And Its Implementation, a report for WWF (UK) by Earth Resources Research, Septemebr 1992.

Yost, N C and Rubin, J W (1993), The National Environmental Policy Act, Law of Environmental Protection, Vol. II, Chapter 9, Environmental Law Institute.

APPENDIX 1

TEXT OF EC DIRECTIVE 85/337/EEC ON ENVIRONMENTAL IMPACT ASSESSMENT

COUNCIL DIRECTIVE
of 27 June 1985
on the assessment of the effects of certain public and private projects on the environment

(85/337/EEC)

THE COUNCIL OF THE EUROPEAN COMMUNITIES,
Having regard to the Treaty establishing the European Economic Community, and in particular Articles 100 and 235 thereof,
Having regard to the proposal from the Commission
Having regard to the opinion of the European Parliament,
Having regard to the opinion of the Economic and Social Committee,
Whereas the 1973 and 1977 action programmes of the European Communities on the environment, as well as the 1983 action programme, the main outlines of which have been approved by the Council of the European Communities and the representatives of the Governments of the Member States, stress that the best environmental policy consists in preventing the creation of pollution or nuisances at source, rather than subsequently trying to counteract their effects; whereas they affirm the need to take effects on the environment into account at the earliest possible stage in all the technical planning and decision-making processes; whereas to that end, they provide for the implementation of procedures to evaluate such effects;
Whereas the disparities between the laws in force in the various Member States with regard to the assessment of the environmental effects of public and private projects may create unfavourable competitive conditions and thereby directly affect the functioning of the common market; whereas, therefore, it is necessary to approximate national laws in this field pursuant to Article 100 of the Treaty;
Whereas, in addition, it is necessary to achieve one of the Community's objectives in the sphere of the protection of the environment and the quality of life;
Whereas, since the Treaty has not provided the powers required for this end, recourse should be had to Article 235 of the Treaty;
Whereas general principles for the assessment of environmental effects should be introduced with a view to supplementing and coordinating development consent procedures governing public and private projects likely to have a major effect on the environment;
Whereas development consent for public and private projects which are likely to have significant effects on the environment should be granted only after prior assessment of the likely significant environmental effects of these projects has been carried out; whereas this assessment must be conducted on the basis

of the appropriate information supplied by the developer, which may be supplemented by the authorities and by the people who may be concerned by the project in question;

Whereas the principles of the assessment of environmental effects should be harmonized, in particular with reference to the projects which should be subject to assessment, the main obligations of the developers and the content of the assessment;

Whereas projects belonging to certain types have significant effects on the environment and these projects must as a rule be subject to systematic assessment;

Whereas projects of other types may not have significant effects on the environment in every case and whereas these projects should be assessed where the Member States consider that their characteristics so require;

Whereas, for projects which are subject to assessment, a certain minimal amount of information must be supplied, concerning the project ant its effects;

Whereas the effects of a project on the environment must be assessed in order to take account of concerns to protect human health, to contribute by means of a better environment to the quality of life, to ensure maintenance of the diversity of species and to maintain the reproductive capacity of the ecosystem as a basic resource for life;

Whereas, however, this Directive should not be applied to projects the details of which are adopted by a specific act of national legislation, since the objectives of this Directive, including that of supplying information, are achieved through the legislative process;

Whereas, furthermore, it may be appropriate in exceptional cases to exempt a specific project from the assessment procedures laid down by this Directive subject to appropriate information being supplied to the Commission,

HAS ADOPTED THIS DIRECTIVE:

Article 1

1. This Directive shall apply to the assessment of the environmental effects of those public and private projects which are likely to have significant effects on the environment.

2. For the purposes of this Directive:

'project' means

- the execution of construction works or of other installations or schemes,
- other interventions in the natural surroundings and landscape including those involving the extraction of mineral resources;

'developer' means:

the applicant for authorization for a private project or the public authority which initiates a project;

'development consent' means:

the decision of the competent authority or authorities which entitles the developer to proceed with the project.

3. The competent authority or authorities shall be that or those which the Member States designate as responsible for performing the duties arising from this Directive.

4. Projects serving national defence purposes are not covered by this Directive.
5. This Directive shall not apply to projects the details of which are adopted by a specific act of national legislation, since the objectives of this Directive, including that of supplying information, are achieved through the legislative process.

Article 2
1. Member States shall adopt all measures necessary to ensure that, before consent is given, projects likely to have significant effects on the environment by virtue inter alia, of their nature, size or location are made subject to an assessment with regard to their effects.
These projects are defined in Article 4
2. The environmental impact assessment may be integrated into the existing procedures for consent to projects in the Member States, or, failing this, into other procedures or into procedures to be established to comply with the aims of this Directive.
3. Member States may, in exceptional cases, exempt a specific project in whole or in part from the provisions laid down in this Directive.
In this event, the Member States shall:
(a) consider whether another form of assessment would be appropriate and whether the information thus collected should be made available to the public;
(b) make available to the public concerned the information relating to the exemption and the reasons for granting it;
(c) inform the Commission, prior to granting consent, of the reasons justifying the exemption granted, and provide it with the information made available, where appropriate, to their own nationals.
The Commission shall immediately forward the documents received to the other Member States.
The Commission shall report annually to the Council on the application of this paragraph.

Article 3
The environmental impact assessment will identify, describe and assess in an appropriate manner, in the light of each individual case and in accordance with the Articles 4 to 11, the direct and indirect effects of a project on the following factors:
- human beings, fauna and flora,
- soil, water, air, climate and the landscape,
- the inter-action between the factors mentioned in the first and second indents,
- material assets and the cultural heritage.

Article 4
1. Subject to Article 2 (3), projects of the classes listed in Annex I shall be made subject to an assessment in accordance with Articles 5 to 10.
2. Projects of the classes listed in Annex II shall be made subject to an assessment, in accordance with Articles 5 to 10, where Member States consider that their characteristics so require.
To this end Member States may inter alia specify certain types of projects as being subject to an assessment or may establish the criteria and/or thresholds

necessary to determine which of the projects of the classes listed in Annex II are to be subject to an assessment in accordance with Articles 5 to 10.

Article 5

1. In the case of projects which, pursuant to Article 4, must be subjected to an environmental impact assessment in accordance with Articles 5 to 10, Member States shall adopt the necessary measures to ensure that the developer supplies in an appropriate form the information specified in Annex III inasmuch as:

(a) the Member States consider that the information is relevant to a given stage of the consent procedure and to the specific characteristics of a particular project or type of project and of the environmental features likely to be affected;

(b) the Member States consider that a developer may reasonably be required to compile this information having regard inter alia to current knowledge and methods of assessment.

2. The information to be provided by the developer in accordance with paragraph 1 shall include at least:

- a description of the project comprising information on the site, design and size of the project,

- a description of the measures envisaged in order to avoid, reduce and, if possible, remedy significant adverse effects,

- the data required to identify and assess the main effects which the project is likely to have on the environment,

- a non-technical summary of the information mentioned in indents 1 to 3.

3. Where they consider it necessary, Member States shall ensure that any authorities with relevant information in their possession make this information available to the developer.

Article 6

1. Member States shall take the measures necessary to ensure that the authorities likely to be concerned by the project by reason of their specific environmental responsibilities are given an opportunity to express their opinion on the request for development consent. Member States shall designate the authorities to be consulted for this purpose in general terms or in each case when the request for consent is made. The information gathered pursuant to Article 5 shall be forwarded to these authorities. Detailed arrangements for consultation shall be laid down by the Member States.

2. 'Member States shall ensure that:

- any request for development consent and any information gathered pursuant to Article 5 are made available to the public,

- the public concerned is given the opportunity to express an opinion before the project is initiated.

3. The detailed arrangements for such information and consultation shall be determined by the Member States, which may in particular, depending on the particular characteristics of the projects or sites concerned:

- determine the public concerned,

- specify the places where the information can be consulted,

- specify the way in which the public may be informed, for example by bill-posting within a certain radius, publication in local newspapers, organization

of exhibitions with plans, drawings, tables, graphs, models,
- determine the manner in which the public is to be consulted, for example, by written submissions, by public enquiry,
- fix appropriate time limits for the various stages of the procedure in order to ensure that a decision is taken within a reasonable period.

Article 7

Where a Member State is aware that a project is likely to have significant effects on the environment in another Member State or where a Member State likely to be significantly affected so requests, the Member State in whose territory the project is intended to be carried out shall forward the information gathered pursuant to Article 5 to the other Member State at the same time as it makes it available to its own nationals. Such information shall serve as a basis for any consultations necessary in the framework of the bilateral relations between two Member States on a reciprocal and equivalent basis.

Article 8

Information gathered pursuant to Articles 5, 6 and 7 must be taken into consideration in the development consent procedure.

Article 9

When a decision has been taken, the competent authority or authorities shall inform the public concerned of:
- the content of the decision and any conditions attached thereto,
- the reasons and considerations on which the decision is based where the Member States' legislation so provides.

The detailed arrangements for such information shall be determined by the Member States.

If another Member State has been informed pursuant to Article 7, it will also be informed of the decision in question.

Article 10

The provisions of this Directive shall not affect the obligation on the competent authorities to respect the limitations imposed by national regulations and administrative provisions and accepted legal practices with regard to industrial and commercial secrecy and the safeguarding of the public interest. Where Article 7 applies, the transmission of information to another Member State and the reception of information by another Member State shall be subject to the limitations in force in the Member State in which the project is proposed.

Article 11

1. The Member States and the Commission shall exchange information on the experience gained in applying this Directive.

2. In particular, Member States shall inform the Commission of any criteria and/or thresholds adopted for the selection of the projects in question, in accordance with Article 4 (2), or of the types of projects concerned which, pursuant to Article 4 (2), are subject to assessment in accordance with Articles

5 to 10.

3. Five years after notification of this Directive, the Commission shall send the European Parliament and the Council a report on its application and effectiveness. The report shall be based on the aforementioned exchange of information.

4. On the basis of this exchange of information, the Commission shall submit to the Council additional proposals, should this be necessary, with a view to this Directive's being applied in a sufficiently coordinated manner.

Article 12

1. Member States shall take the measures necessary to comply with this Directive within three years of its notification (1).

2. Member States shall communicate to the Commission the texts of the provisions of national law which they adopt in the field covered by this Directive.

Article 13

The provisions of this Directive shall not affect the right of Member States to lay down stricter rules regarding scope and procedure when assessing environmental effects.

Article 14

This Directive is addressed to the Member States.

Done at Luxembourg, 27 June 1985.

(1) This Directive was notified to the Member States on 3 July 1985.

ANNEX I
PROJECTS SUBJECT TO ARTICLE 4 (1)

1. Crude-oil refineries (excluding undertakings manufacturing only lubricants from crude oil) and installations for the gasification and liquefaction of 500 tonnes or more of coal or bituminous shale per day.

2. Thermal power stations and other combustion installations with a heat output of 300 megawatts or more and nuclear power stations and other nuclear reactors (except research installations for the production and conversion of fissionable and fertile materials, whose maximum power does not exceed I kilowatt continuous thermal load).

3. Installations solely designed for the permanent storage or final disposal of radioactive waste.

4. Integrated works for the initial melting of cast-iron and steel.

5. Installations for the extraction of asbestos and for the processing and transformation of asbestos and products containing asbestos: for asbestos-cement products, with an annual production of more than 20 000 tonnes of finished products, for friction material, with an annual production of more than 50 tonnes of finished products, and for other uses of asbestos, utilization of more than 200 tonnes per year.

6. Integrated chemical installations.

7. Construction of motorways, express roads (1) and lines for long-distance railway traffic and of airports(2) with a basic runway length of 2 100 m or more.

8. Trading ports and also inland waterways and ports for inland-waterway traffic which permit the passage of vessels of over 1 350 tonnes.

9. Waste-disposal installations for the incineration, chemical treatment or

land fill of toxic and dangerous wastes.

[1]For the purposes of the Directive, 'express road' means a road which complies with the definition in the European Agreement on main international traffic arteries of 15 November 1975.
[2]For the purposes of this Directive, 'airport' means airports which comply with the definition in the 1944 Chicago Convention setting up the International Civil Aviation Organization (Annex 14).

ANNEX II

PROJECTS SUBJECT TO ARTICLE 4 (2)

1. Agriculture
(a) Projects for the restructuring of rural land holdings.
(b) Projects for the use of uncultivated land or semi-natural areas for intensive agricultural purposes.
(c) Water-management projects for agriculture.
(d) Initial afforestation where this may lead to adverse ecological changes and land reclamation for the purposes of conversion to another type of land use.
(e) Poultry-rearing installations.
(f) Pig-rearing installations.
(g) Salmon breeding.
(h) Reclamation of land from the sea.

2. Extractive industry
(a) Extraction of peat.
(b) Deep drillings with the exception of drillings for investigating the stability of the soil and in particular: - geothermal drilling,
  - drilling for the storage of nuclear waste material,
  - drilling for water supplies.
(c) Extraction of minerals other than metalliferous and energy-producing minerals, such as marble, sand, gravel, shale, salt, phosphates and potash.
(d) Extraction of coal and lignite by underground mining.

(e) Extraction of coal and lignite by open-cast mining.

(f) Extraction of petroleum.

(g) Extraction of natural gas.

(h) Extraction of ores.

(i) Extraction of bituminous shale.

(j) Extraction of minerals other than metalliferous and energy-producing minerals by opencast mining.

(k) Surface industrial installations for the extraction of coal, petroleum, natural gas and ores, as well as bituminous shale.

(l) Coke ovens (dry coal distillation).

(m) Installations for the manufacture of cement.

3. Energy industry

(a) Industrial installations for the production of electricity, steam and hot water (unless included in Annex I).

(b) Industrial installations for carrying gas, steam and hot water; transmission of electrical energy by overhead cables.

(c) Surface storage of natural gas.

(d) Underground storage of combustible gases.

(e) Surface storage of fossil fuels.

(f) Industrial briquetting of coal and lignite.

(g) Installations for the production or enrichment of nuclear fuels.

(h) Installations for the reprocessing of irradiated nuclear fuels.

(i) Installations for the collection and processing of radioactive waste (unless included in Annex I).

(j) Installations for hydroelectric energy production.

4. Processing of metals

(a) Iron and steelworks, including foundries, forges, drawing plants and rolling mills (unless included in Annex I).

(b) Installations for the production, including smelting, refining, drawing and rolling, of non-ferrous metals, excluding precious metals.

(c) Pressing, drawing and stamping of large castings.

(d) Surface treatment and coating of metals.

(e) Boilermaking, manufacture of reservoirs, tanks and other sheet-metal container.

(f) Manufacture and assembly of motor vehicles and manufacture of motor-vehicle engines.

(g) Shipyards.

(h) Installations for the construction and repair of aircraft.

(i) Manufacture of railway equipment.

(j) Swaging by explosives.

(k) Installations for the roasting and sintering of metallic ores.

5. Manufacture of glass

6. Chemical industry

(a) Treatment of intermediate products and production of chemicals (unless included in Annex I).

(b) Production of pesticides and pharmaceutical products, paint and varnishes, elastomers and peroxides.

(c) Storage facilities for petroleum, petrochemical and chemical products.

7. Food industry

(a) Manufacture of vegetable and animal oils and fats.

(b) Packing and canning of animal and vegetable products.

(c) Manufacture of dairy products.

(d) Brewing and malting.

(e) Confectionery and syrup manufacture.

(f) Installations for the slaughter of animals.

(g) Industrial starch manufacturing installations.

(h) Fish-meal and fish-oil factories.

(i) Sugar factories.

8. Textile, leather, wood and paper industries

(a) Wool scouring, degreasing and bleaching factories.

(b) Manufacture of fibre board, particle board and plywood.

(c) Manufacture of pulp, paper and board.

(d) Fibre-dyeing factories.

(e) Cellulose-processing and production installations.

(f) Tannery and leather-dressing factories.

9. Rubber industry

Manufacture and treatment of elastomer-based products.

10. Infrastructure projects

(a) Industrial-estate development projects.

(b) Urban-development projects.

(c) Ski-lifts and cable cars.

(d) Construction of roads, harbours, including fishing harbours, and airfields (projects not listed in Annex I).

(e) Canalization and flood-relief works.

(f) Dams and other installations designed to hold water or store it on a long-term basis.

(g) Tramways, elevated and underground railways, suspended lines or similar lines of a particular type, used exclusively or mainly for passenger transport.

(h) Oil and gas pipeline installations.

(i) Installation of long-distance aqueducts.

(j) Yacht marinas.

11. Other projects

(a) Holiday villages, hotel complexes.
(b) Permanent racing and test tracks for cars and motor cycles.

(c) Installations for the disposal of industrial and domestic waste (unless included in Annex I).

(d) Waste water treatment plants.

(e) Sludge-deposition sites.

(f) Storage of scrap iron.

(g) Test benches for engines, turbines or reactors.

(h) Manufacture of artificial mineral fibres.

(i) Manufacture, packing, loading or placing in cartridges of gunpowder and explosives.

(j) Knackers' yards.

12. Modifications to development projects included in Annex I and projects in Annex I undertaken exclusively or mainly for the development and testing of new methods or products and not used for more than one year.

ANNEX III
INFORMATION REFERRED TO IN ARTICLE 5 (I)

1. Description of the project, including in particular:

- a description of the physical characteristics of the whole project and the land-use requirements during the construction and operational phases,

- a description of the main characteristics of the production processes, for instance, nature and quantity of the materials used,

- an estimate, by type and quantity, of expected residues and emissions (water, air and soil pollution, noise, vibration, light, heat, radiation, etc) resulting from the operation of the proposed project.

2. Where appropriate, an outline of the main alternatives studied by the developer and an indication of the main reasons for his choice, taking into account the environmental effects.

3. A description of the aspects of the environment likely to be significantly affected by the proposed project, including in particular, population, fauna, flora, soil, water, air, climatic factors, material assets, including the architectural and archaeological heritage, landscape and the inter-relationship between the above factors.

4. A description ([1]) of the likely significant effects of the proposed project on the environment resulting from:

- the existence of the project,

- the use of natural resources,

-the emission of pollutants, the creation of nuisances and the elimination of waste;

and the description by the developer of the forecasting methods used to assess the effects on the environment.

5. A description of the measures envisaged to prevent, reduce and where possible offset any significant adverse effects on the environment.

6. A non-technical summary of the information provided under the above headings.

7. An indication of any difficulties (technical deficiencies or lack of know-how) encountered by the developer in compiling the required information.

([1]) The description should cover the direct effects and any indirect, secondary, cumulative, short, medium and long-term, permanent and temporary, positive and negative effects of the project.

APPENDIX 2

TEXT OF UNECE (ESPOO) CONVENTION ON TRANSBOUNDARY IMPACTS

CONVENTION
on Environmental Impact Assessment in a Transboundary Context

THE PARTIES TO THIS CONVENTION,

AWARE of the interrelationship between economic activities and their environmental consequences,

AFFIRMING the need to ensure environmentally sound and sustainable development,

DETERMINED to enhance international co-operation in assessing environmental impact in particular in a transboundary context,

MINDFUL of the need and importance to develop anticipatory policies and of preventing, mitigating and monitoring significant adverse environmental impact in general and more specifically in a transboundary context,

RECALLING the relevant provisions of the Charter of the United Nations, the Declaration of the Stockholm Conference on the Human Environment, the Final Act of the Conference on Security and Cooperation in Europe (CSCE) and the Concluding Documents of the Madrid and Vienna Meetings of Representatives of the Participating States of the CSCE,

COMMENDING the ongoing activities of States to ensure that, through their national legal and administrative provisions and their national policies, environmental impact assessment is carried out,

CONSCIOUS of the need to give explicit consideration to environmental factors at an early stage in the decision making process by applying environmental impact assessment, at all appropriate administrative levels, as a necessary tool to improve the quality of information presented to decision makers so that environmentally sound decisions can be made paying careful attention to minimizing significant adverse impact, particularly in a transboundary context,

MINDFUL of the efforts of international organisations to promote the use of environmental impact assessment both at the national and international levels, and taking into account work on environmental impact assessment carried out under the auspices of the United Nations Economic Commission for Europe, in particular results achieved by the Seminar on Environmental

Impact Assessment (September 1987, Warsaw, Poland) as well as noting the Goals and Principles on environmental impact assessment adopted by the Governing Council of the United Nations Environment Programme, and the Ministerial Declaration on Sustainable Development (May 1990, Bergen, Norway),

HAVE AGREED AS FOLLOWS:

Article 1
Definitions

1. 'Parties' means, unless the text otherwise indicates, the Contracting Parties to this Convention;

2. 'Party of origin' means the Contracting Party or Parties to this Convention under whose jurisdiction a proposed activity is envisaged to take place;

3. 'Affected Party' means the Contracting Party or Parties to this Convention likely to be affected by the transboundary impact of a proposed activity;

4. 'Concerned Parties' means the Party of origin and the affected Party of an environmental impact assessment pursuant to the Convention;

5. 'Proposed activity' means any activity or any major change to an activity subject to a decision of a competent authority in accordance with an applicable national procedure;

6. 'Environmental impact assessment' means a national procedure for evaluating the likely impact of a proposed activity on the environment;

7. 'Impact' means any effect caused by a proposed activity on the environment including human health and safety, flora, fauna, soil, air, water, climate, landscape and historical monuments or other physical structures or the interaction among these factors; it also includes effects on cultural heritage or socio-economic conditions resulting from alterations to those factors;

8. 'Transboundary impact' means any impact, not exclusively of a global nature, within an area under the jurisdiction of a Party caused by a proposed activity the physical origin of which is situated wholly or in part within the area under the jurisdiction of another Party;

9. 'Competent authority' means the national authority or authorities designated by a Party as responsible for performing the tasks covered by this Convention and/or the authority or authorities entrusted by a Party with decision making powers regarding the proposed activity;

10. 'The Public' means one or more natural or legal persons.

Article 2
General provisions

1. The parties shall, either individually or jointly, take all appropriate and effective measures to prevent, reduce and control significant adverse transboundary environmental impact from proposed activities.

2. Each Party shall take the necessary legal, administrative or other measures to implement the provisions of this Convention, including, with respect to proposed activities listed in Appendix I that are likely to cause significant adverse transboundary impact, the establishment of an environmental impact assessment procedure that permits public participation and preparation of the environmental impact assessment documentation described in Appendix II.

3. The Party of origin shall ensure that in accordance with the provisions of this Convention an environmental impact assessment is undertaken prior to a decision to authorize or undertake a proposed activity listed in Appendix I that is likely to cause a significant adverse transboundary impact.

4. The Party of origin shall, consistent with the provisions of this Convention, ensure that affected parties are notified of a proposed activity listed in Appendix I that is likely to cause a significant adverse transboundary impact.

5. Concerned Parties shall, at the initiative of any such party, enter into discussion on whether one or more proposed activities not listed in Appendix I is or are likely to cause a significant adverse transboundary impact and thus should be treated as if it or they were so listed. Where those Parties so agree, the activity or activities shall be thus treated. General guidance for identifying criteria to determine significant adverse impact is set forth in Appendix III.

6. The Party of origin shall provide, in accordance with the provisions of this Convention, an opportunity to the public in the areas likely to be affected to participate in relevant environmental impact assessment procedures regarding the proposed activities and shall ensure that the opportunity provided to the public of the affected Party is equivalent to that provided to the public of the Party of origin.

7. Environmental impact assessments as required by this Convention shall, as a minimum requirement, be undertaken at the project level of the proposed activity. To the extent appropriate, the Parties shall endeavour to apply the principles of environmental impact assessment to policies, plans and programmes.

8. The provisions of this Convention shall not affect the right of Parties to implement national laws, regulations, administrative provisions or accepted legal practices protecting information the supply of which would be prejudicial to industrial and commercial secrecy or national security.

9. The provisions of this Convention shall not affect the right of particular Parties to implement, by bilateral or multilateral agreement where appropriate, more stringent measures than those of this Convention.

10. The provisions of this Convention shall not prejudice any obligations of the parties under international law with regard to activities having or likely to have a transboundary impact.

Article 3
Notification

1. For a proposed activity listed in Appendix I that is likely to cause a significant adverse transboundary impact, the Party of origin shall, for the purposes of ensuring adequate and effective consultations pursuant to Article 5, notify any party which it considers may be an affected Party as early as possible and no later than when informing its own public about that proposed activity.

2. This notification shall contain, inter alia:

(a) information on the proposed activity, including any available information on its possible transboundary impact;

(b) the nature of the possible decision; and

(c) an indication of a reasonable time within which a response under paragraph 3 of this Article is required, taking into account the nature of the proposed activity;

and may include the information set out in paragraph 5 of this Article.

3. The affected Party shall respond to the party of origin within the time specified in the notification, acknowledging receipt of the notification, and shall indicate whether it intends to participate in the environmental impact assessment procedure.

4. If the affected Party indicates that it does not intend to participate in the environmental impact assessment procedure, or if it does not respond within the time specified in the notification, the provisions in paragraphs 5, 6, 7 and 8 of this Article and in Articles 4 to 7 will not apply. In such circumstances the right of a Party of origin to determine whether to carry out an environmental impact assessment on the basis of its national law and practice is not prejudiced.

5. Upon receipt of a response from the affected Party indicating its desire to participate in the environmental impact assessment procedure, the Party of origin shall, if it has not already done so, provide to the affected Party:

(a) relevant information regarding the environmental impact assessment procedure, including an indication of the time schedule for transmittal of comments; and

(b) relevant information on the proposed activity and its possible significant adverse transboundary impact.

6. An affected Party shall, at the request of the Party of origin, provide the latter with reasonably obtainable information relating to the potentially affected environment under the jurisdiction of the affected Party, where such information is necessary for the preparation of the environmental impact assessment documentation. The information shall be furnished promptly and, as appropriate, through a joint body where one exists.

7. When a Party considers that it would be affected by significant adverse transboundary impact of a proposed activity listed in Appendix I, and when no notification has taken place in accordance with paragraph 1 of this Article, the concerned Parties shall, at the request of the affected Party, exchange sufficient information for the purposes of holding discussions on whether there is likely to be a significant adverse transboundary impact. If those Parties agree that there is likely to be a significant adverse transboundary impact, the provisions of this Convention shall apply accordingly. If those Parties cannot agree whether there is likely to be a significant adverse transboundary impact, any such Party may submit that question to an inquiry commission in accordance with the provisions of Appendix IV to advise on the likelihood of significant adverse transboundary impact, unless they agree on another method of settling the question.

8. The concerned parties shall ensure that the public of the affected Party in the areas likely to be affected be informed of, and be provided with possibilities for making comments or objections on, the proposed activity, and for the transmittal of these comments or objections to the competent authority of the Party of origin, either directly to this authority or, where appropriate, through the Party of origin.

Article 4
Preparation of the environmental impact assessment documentation

1. The environmental impact assessment documentation to be submitted to the competent authority of the Party of origin shall contain, as a minimum, the information described in Appendix II.

2. The Party of origin shall furnish the affected Party, as appropriate through a joint body where one exists, with the environmental impact assessment documentation. The concerned Parties shall arrange for distribution of the documentation to the authorities and the public of the affected Party in the areas likely to be affected and for the submission of comments to the competent

authority of the Party of origin, either directly to this authority or, where appropriate, through the Party of origin within a reasonable time before the final decision is taken on the proposed activity.

Article 5
Consultations on the basis of the environmental impact assessment documentation

The Party of origin shall, after completion of the environmental impact assessment documentation, without undue delay enter into consultations with the affected Party concerning, inter alia, the potential transboundary impact of the proposed activity and measures to reduce or eliminate its impacts. Consultations may relate to:

(a) possible alternatives to the proposed activity, including the no-action alternative and possible measures to mitigate significant adverse transboundary impact and to monitor the effects of such measures at the expense of the party of origin;

(b) other forms of possible mutual assistance in reducing any significant adverse transboundary impact of the proposed activity; and

(c) any other appropriate matters relating to the proposed activity.

The Parties shall agree, at the commencement of such consultations, on a reasonable time-frame for the duration of the consultation period. Any such consultations may be conducted through an appropriate joint body, where one exists.

Article 6
Final decision
1. The parties shall ensure that, in the final decision on the proposed activity, due account is taken of the outcome of the environmental impact assessment, including the environmental impact assessment documentation, as well as the comments thereon received pursuant to Article 3 (8) and Article 4 (2) and the outcome of the consultation as referred to in Article 5.

2. The Party of origin shall provide to the affected party the final decision on the proposed activity along with the reasons and considerations on which it was based.

3. if additional information on the significant transboundary impact of a proposed activity, which was not available at the time a decision was made with respect to that activity and which could have materially affected the decision, becomes available to a concerned Party before work on that activity commences, that Party shall immediately inform the other concerned Party

or Parties. If one of the concerned Parties so requests, consultations shall be held as to whether the decision needs to be revised.

Article 7
Post-project analysis

1. The concerned Parties, at the request of any such party, shall determine whether, and if so to what extent, a post-project analysis shall be carried out, taking into account the likely significant adverse transboundary impact of the activity for which an environmental impact assessment has been undertaken pursuant to this Convention. Any post-project analysis undertaken shall include, in particular, the surveillance of the activity and the determination of any adverse transboundary impact. Such surveillance and determination may be undertaken with a view to achieving the objectives listed in Appendix V.

2. When, as a result of post-project analysis, the Party of origin or the affected Party has reasonable grounds for concluding that there is a significant adverse transboundary impact or factors have been discovered which may result in such an impact, it shall immediately inform the other Party. The concerned Parties shall then consult on necessary measures to reduce or eliminate the impact.

Article 8
Bilateral and multilateral cooperation

The Parties may continue existing or enter into new bilateral or multilateral agreements or other arrangements in order to implement their obligations under this Convention. Such agreements or other arrangements may be based on the elements listed in Appendix VI.

Article 9

Research programmes

The Parties shall give special consideration to the setting up, or intensification of, specific research programmes aimed at:
(a) improving existing qualitative and quantitative methods for assessing the impacts of proposed activities;

(b) achieving a better understanding of cause-effect relationships and their role in integrated environmental management;

(c) analysing and monitoring the efficient implementation of decisions on proposed activities with the intention of minimizing or preventing impacts;

(d) developing methods to stimulate creative approaches in the search for environmentally sound alternatives to proposed activities, production and consumption patterns;

(e) developing methodologies for the application of the principles of environmental impact assessment at the macro-economic level.

The results of the programmes listed above shall be exchanged by the Parties.

Article 10
Status of the appendices
The Appendices attached to this Convention form an integral part of the Convention.
Article 11
Meeting of Parties

1. The Parties shall meet, so far as possible, in connection with the annual sessions of the senior advisers to ECE Governments on environmental and water problems. The first meeting of the Parties shall be convened not later than one year after the date of the entry into force of this Convention. Thereafter, meetings of the Parties shall be held at such other times as may be deemed necessary by a meeting of the parties, or at the written request of any Party, provided that, within six months of the request being communicated to them by the secretariat, it is supported by at least one third of the Parties.

2. Except as provided for in paragraph 1 of this Article, regional economic integration organisations, in matters within their competence, shall exercise their right to vote with a number of votes equal to the number of their member States which are parties to this Convention. Such organisations shall not exercise their right to vote if their member States exercise theirs, and vice versa.

Article 13
Secretariat

The Executive Secretary of the Economic Commission for Europe shall carry out the following secretariat functions:

(a) the convening and preparing of meetings of the parties;

(b) the transmission of reports and other information received in accordance with the provisions of this Convention to the Parties; and

(c) the performance of other functions as may be provided for in this Convention or as may be determined by the Parties.

Article 14

Amendments to the Convention

1. Any Party may propose amendments to this Convention.

2. Proposed amendments shall be submitted in writing to the secretariat, which shall communicate them to all Parties. The proposed amendments shall be discussed at the next meeting of the parties, provided these proposals have been circulate by the secretariat to the Parties at least ninety days in advance.

3. The Parties shall make every effort to reach agreement on any proposed amendment to this Convention by consensus. If all efforts at consensus have been exhausted, and no agreement reached, the amendment shall as a last resort be adopted by a three-fourths majority vote of the Parties present and voting at the meeting.

4. Amendments to this Convention adopted in accordance with paragraph 3 of this Article shall be submitted by the depositary to all Parties for ratification, approval or acceptance. They shall enter into force for parties having ratified, approved or accepted them on the 90th day after the receipt by the depositary of notification of their ratification, approval or acceptance by at last three-fourths of these Parties. Thereafter they shall enter into force for any other party on the ninetieth day after that party deposits its instruments of ratification, approval or acceptance of the amendments.

5. For the purpose of this Article, 'Parties present voting' means parties present and casting an affirmative or negative vote.

6. The voting procedure set forth in paragraph 3 of this Article is not intended to constitute a precedent for future agreements negotiated within the Economic Commission for Europe.

Article 15
Settlement of disputes

1. If a dispute arises between two or more Parties about the interpretation or application of this Convention, they shall seek a solution by negotiation or by any other method of dispute settlement acceptable to the parties to the dispute.

2. When signing, ratifying, accepting, approving or acceding to this Convention, or at any time thereafter, a Party may declare in writing to the Depositary that for a dispute not resolved in accordance with paragraph 1 of this Article, it accepts one or both of the following means of dispute settlement as compulsory in relation to any Party accepting the same obligation:
(a) submission of the dispute to the International Court of Justice;
(b) arbitration in accordance with the procedure set out in Appendix VII.
3. If the parties to the dispute have accepted both means of dispute settlement

referred to in paragraph 2 of this Article, the dispute may be submitted only to the International Court of Justice, unless the parties agree otherwise.

Article 16
Signature

This Convention shall be open for signature at Espoo (Finland) from 25 February to 1 March 1991 and thereafter at United Nations Headquarters in New York until 2 September 1991 by States members of the Economic Commission for Europe as well as States having consultative status with the Economic Commission for Europe pursuant to paragraph 8 of the Economic and Social Council resolution 36 (IV) of 28 March 1947, and by regional economic integration organisations constituted by sovereign States members of the Economic Commission for Europe to which their member States have transferred competence in respect of matters governed by this Convention, including the competence to enter into treaties in respect of these matters.

Article 17
Ratification, acceptance, approval and accession

1. This Convention shall be subject to ratification, acceptance or approval by signatory States and regional economic integration organisations.
2. This Convention shall be open for accession as from 3 September 1991 by the States and organisations referred to in Article 16.

3. The instruments of ratification, acceptance, approval or accession shall be deposited with the Secretary-General of the United Nations, who shall perform the functions of Depositary.

4. Any organisation referred to in Article 16 which becomes a Party to this Convention without any of its member States being a Party shall be bound by all the obligations under this Convention. In the case of such organisations, one or more of whose member States is a Party to this Convention, the organisation and its member States shall decide on their respective responsibilities for the performance of their obligations under this Convention. In such cases, the organisation and the member States shall not be entitled to exercise rights under this Convention concurrently.

5. In their instruments of ratification, acceptance, approval or accession; the regional economic integration organisations referred to in Article 16 shall declare the extent of their competence with respect to the matters governed by this Convention. These organisations shall also inform the Depositary of any relevant modification to the extent of their competence.
Article 18
Entry into force

1. This Convention shall enter into force on the ninetieth day after the date of deposit of the 16th instrument of ratification, acceptance, approval or accession.

2. For the purposes of paragraph 1 of this Article, any instrument deposited by a regional economic integration organisation shall not be counted as additional to those deposited by States members of such an organisation.

3. For each State or organisation referred to in Article 16 which ratifies, accepts or approves this Convention or accedes thereto after the deposit of the sixteenth instrument of ratification, acceptance, approval or accession, this Convention shall enter into force on the ninetieth day after the deposit by such State or organisation of its instrument of ratification, acceptance, approval or accession.

Article 19
Withdrawal

At any time after four years from the date on which this Convention has come into force with respect to a Party, that Party may withdraw from this Convention by giving written notification to the depositary. Any such withdrawal shall take effect on the 90th day after the date of its receipt by the depositary. Any such withdrawal shall not affect the application of Articles 3 to 6 of this Convention to a proposed activity in or a request has been made pursuant to Article 3 (7) before such withdrawal took effect.

Article 20
Authentic texts

The original of this Convention, of which the English, French and Russian texts are equally authentic, shall be deposited with the Secretary-General of the United Nations.

IN WITNESS WHEREOF the undersigned, being duly authorised thereto, have signed this Convention.

DONE at Espoo (Finland), this twenty-fifth day of February one thousand nine hundred and ninety-one.

APPENDIX I

List of activities

1. Crude oil refineries (excluding undertakings manufacturing only lubricants from crude oil) and installations for the gasification and liquefaction of 500 tonnes or more of coal or bituminous shale per day.

2. thermal power station and other combustion installations with a heat output of 300 megawatts or more and nuclear power station and other nuclear reactors (except research installations for the production and conversion of fissionable and fertile materials, whose maximum power does not exceed 1 kilowatt continuous load).

3. Installations solely designed for the production or enrichment of nuclear fuels, for the reprocessing of irradiated nuclear fuels or for the storage, disposal and processing of radioactive waste.

4. Major installations for the initial smelting of cast-iron and steel and for the production of non-ferrous metals.

5. Installations for the extraction of asbestos and for the processing and transformation of asbestos and products containing asbestos; for asbestos-cement products, with an annual production of more than 20 000 tonnes finished product; for friction material, with an annual production of more than 50 tonnes finished product; and for other asbestos utilisation of more than 200 tonnes per year.

6. Integrated chemical installations.

7. Construction of motorways, express roads, and lines for long-distance railway traffic and of airports with a basic runway length of 2 100 metres or more.([1])

8. Large-diameter oil and gas pipelines.

9. Trading ports and also inland waterways and ports for inland-waterway traffic which permit the passage of vessels of over 1 350 tonnes.

10. Waste-disposal installations for the incineration, chemical treatment or landfill of toxic and dangerous wastes.

11. Large dams and reservoirs.

12. Groundwater abstraction activities in cases where the annual volume of water to be abstracted amounts to 10 million cubic metres or more.

13. Pulp and paper manufacturing of 200 air-dried metric tonnes or more per day.

14. Major mining, on-site extraction and processing of metal ores or coal.

15. Offshore hydrocarbon production.

16. Major storage facilities for petroleum, petrochemical and chemical products.

17. Deforestation of large areas.

(¹) For the purposes of this Convention:

- "motorway" means a road specially designed and built for motor traffic, which does not serve properties bordering on it, and which:

(a) is provided, except at special points or temporarily, with separate carriageways for the two directions of traffic, separated from each other by a dividing strip not intended for traffic or, exceptionally, by other means;
(b) does not cross at level with any road, railway or tramway track, or footpath; and

(c) is specially sign-posted as a motorway.

- "express road" means a road reserved for motor traffic accessible only from interchanges or controlled junctions and on which, in particular, stopping and parking are prohibited on the running carriageway(s).

APPENDIX II

Content of the environmental impact assessment documentation

Information to be included in the environmental impact assessment documentation shall as a minimum, contain, in accordance with Article 4:

(a) a description, of the proposed activity and purpose;

(b) a description, where appropriate, of reasonable alternatives (for example, locational or technological) to the proposed activity and also the no-action alternative;

(c) a description of the environment likely to be significantly affected by the proposed activity and its alternatives;

(d) a description of the potential environmental impact of the proposed activity and its alternatives and an estimation of its significance;

(e) a description of mitigation measures to keep adverse environmental impact to a minimum;

(f) an explicit indication of predictive methods and underlying assumptions as well as the relevant environmental data used;

(g) an identification of gaps in knowledge and uncertainties encountered in compiling the required information;

(h) where appropriate, an outline for monitoring and management programmes and any plans for post-project analysis; and

(i) a non-technical summary including a visual presentation as appropriate (maps, graphs, etc.).

APPENDIX III

General criteria to assist in the determination of the environmental significance of activities not listed in Appendix I.

1. In considering proposed activities to which Article 2 (5) applies, the concerned parties may consider whether the activity is likely to have a significant adverse transboundary impact in particular by virtue of one or more of the following criteria:

(a) Size: proposed activities which are large for the type of activity;

(b) Location: proposed activities which are located in or close to an area of special environmental sensitivity or importance (such as wetlands designated under the Ramsar Convention, national parks, nature reserves, sites of special scientific interest, or sites of archaeological, cultural or historical importance); also, proposed activities in locations where the characteristics of the proposed development would be likely to have significant effects on the population;

(c) Effects: proposed activities with particularly complex and potentially adverse effects, including those giving rise to serious effects on humans or valued species or organisms, those which threaten the existing or potential use of an affected area and those causing additional loading which cannot be sustained by the carrying capacity of the environment.

APPENDIX IV

Inquiry procedure

1. The requesting Party or Parties shall notify the secretariat that it or they submit(s) the question of whether a proposed activity listed in Appendix I is likely to have a significant adverse transboundary impact to an inquiry commission established in accordance with the provisions of this Appendix. This notification shall state the subject-matter of the inquiry. The secretariat shall notify immediately all Parties to this Convention of this submission.

2. The inquiry commission shall consist of three members. Both the requesting party and the other Party to the inquiry procedure shall appoint a scientific or technical expert, and the two experts so appointed shall designate by common agreement the third expert, who shall be the president of the inquiry commission. the latter shall not be a national of one of the Parties to the inquiry procedure, nor have his or her usual place of residence in the territory of one these Parties, nor be employed by any of them, nor have dealt with the matter in any other capacity.

3. If the president of the inquiry commission has not been designated within two months of the appointment of the second expert, the Executive Secretary of the Economic Commission for Europe shall, at the request of either Party, designate the president within the further two-month period.

4. If one of the Parties to the inquiry procedure does not appoint an expert within one month of its receipt of the notification by the secretariat, the other Party may inform the Executive Secretary of the Economic Commission for Europe, who shall designate the president of the inquiry commission within a further two-month period. Upon designation, the president of the inquiry commission shall request the party which has not appointed an expert to do so within one month. After such a period, the president shall inform the Executive Secretary to the Economic Commission for Europe, who shall make this appointment within a further two-month period.

5. The inquiry commission shall adopt its own rules of procedure.

6. The inquiry commission may take all appropriate measures in order to carry out its functions.

7. The Parties to the inquiry procedure shall facilitate the work of the inquiry commission and, in particular, using all means at their disposal, shall:

(a) provide it with all relevant documents, facilities and information; and

(b) enable it, where necessary, to call witnesses or experts and receive their evidence.

8. The Parties and the experts shall protect the confidentiality of any information

they receive in confidence during the work of the inquiry commission.

9. If one of the Parties to the inquiry procedures does not appear before the inquiry commission or fails to present its case, the other Party may request the inquiry commission to continue the proceedings and to complete its work. Absence of a Party or failure of a Party to present its case shall not constitute a bar to the continuation and completion of the work of the inquiry commission.

10. Unless the inquiry commission determines otherwise because of the particular circumstances of the matter, the expenses of the inquiry commission, including the remuneration of its members, shall be borne by the Parties to the inquiry procedure in equal shares. The inquiry commission shall keep a record of all its expenses, and shall furnish a final statement thereof to the parties.

11. Any Party having an interest of a factual nature in the subject-matter of the inquiry procedure, and which may be affected by an opinion in the matter may intervene in the proceedings with the consent of the inquiry commission.

12. The decisions of the inquiry commission on matters of procedure shall be taken by majority vote of its members. The final opinion of the inquiry commission shall reflect the view of the majority of its members and shall include any dissenting view.

13. The inquiry commission shall present its final opinion within two months of the date on which it was established unless it finds it necessary to extend this time limit for a period which should not exceed two months.

14. The final opinion of the inquiry commission shall be based on accepted scientific principles. The final opinion shall be transmitted by the inquiry commission to the Parties to the inquiry procedure and to the secretariat.

APPENDIX V

Post-project analysis

Objectives include:

(a) monitoring compliance with the conditions as set out in the authorization or approval of the activity and the effectiveness of mitigation measures;

(b) review of an impact for proper management and in order to cope with uncertainties;

(c) verification of past predictions in order to transfer experience to future activities of the same type.

APPENDIX VI

Elements for bilateral and multilateral co-operation

1. Concerned Parties may set up, where appropriate, institutional arrangements or enlarge the mandate of existing institutional arrangements within the framework of bilateral or multilateral agreements in order to give full effect to this Convention.

2. Bilateral and multilateral agreements or other arrangements may include:

(a) any additional requirements for the implementation of this Convention, taking into account the specific conditions of the subregion concerned;

(b) institutional, administrative and other arrangements, to be made on a reciprocal and equivalent basis;

(c) harmonisation of their policies and measures for the protection of the environment in order to attain the greatest possible similarity in standards and methods related to the implementation of environmental impact assessment;

(d) developing, improving, and/or harmonising methods for the identification, measurement, prediction and assessment of impacts, and for post-project analysis;

(e) developing and/or improving methods and programmes for the collection, analysis, storage and timely dissemination of comparable data regarding environmental quality in order to provide input into the environmental impact assessment;

(f) the establishment of threshold levels and more specified criteria for defining the significance of transboundary impacts related to the location, nature or size of proposed activities, for which environmental impact assessment in accordance with the provisions of this Convention shall be applied; and the establishment of critical loads of transboundary pollution;

(g) undertaking, where appropriate, joint environmental impact assessment, development of joint monitoring programmes, intercalibration of monitoring devices and harmonisation of methodologies with a view to rendering the data and information obtained compatible.

APPENDIX VII

Arbitration

1. The claimant Party or Parties shall notify the secretariat that the Parties have agreed to submit the dispute to arbitration pursuant to Article 15 (2) of this Convention. The notification shall state the subject-matter of arbitration and include, in particular, the Articles of this Convention, the interpretation or application of which are at issue. The secretariat shall forward the information received to all Parties to this Convention.

2. The arbitral tribunal shall consist of three members. Both the claimant Party or Parties and the other party or Parties to the dispute shall appoint an arbitrator, and the two arbitrators so appointed shall designate by common agreement the third arbitrator, who shall be the president of the arbitral tribunal. The latter shall not be a national of one of the Parties to the dispute, nor have his or her usual place of residence in the territory of one of these Parties, nor be employed by any of them, nor have dealt with the case in any other capacity.

3. If the president of the arbitral tribunal has not been designated within two months of the appointment of the second arbitrator, the Executive Secretary of the Economic Commission for Europe shall, at the request of either Party to the dispute, designate the president within a further two-month period.

4. If one of the Parties to the dispute does not appoint an arbitrator within two months of the receipt of the request, the other Party may inform the Executive Secretary of the Economic Commission for Europe, who shall designate the president of the arbitral tribunal within a further two-month period. Upon designation, the president of the arbitral tribunal shall request the party which has not appointed an arbitrator to do so within two months. After such a period, the president shall inform the Executive Secretary of the Economic Commission for Europe, who shall make this appointment within a further two-month period.

5. The arbitral tribunal shall render its decision in accordance with international law and in accordance with the provisions of this Convention.

6. Any arbitral tribunal constituted under the provisions set out herein shall draw up its own rules of procedure.

7. The decisions of the arbitral tribunal, both on procedure and on substance, shall be taken by majority vote of its members.

8. The tribunal may take all appropriate measures in order to establish the facts.

9. The Parties to the dispute shall facilitate the work of the arbitral tribunal and, in particular, using all means at their disposal, shall:
(a) provide it with all relevant documents, facilities and information; and

(b) enable it, where necessary, to call witnesses or experts and receive their evidence.

10. The Parties and the arbitrators shall protect the confidentiality of any information they receive in confidence during the proceedings of the arbitral tribunal.

11. The arbitral tribunal may, at the request of one of the Parties, recommend measures of protection.

12. If one of the Parties to the dispute does not appear before the arbitral tribunal or fails to defend its case, the other Party may request the tribunal to continue the proceedings and to render its final decision. Absence of a Party or failure of a Party to defend its case shall not constitute a bar to the proceedings. Before rendering its final decision, the arbitral tribunal must satisfy itself that the claim is well founded in fact and law.

13. The arbitral tribunal may hear and determine counter-claims arising directly out of the subject-matter of the dispute.

14. Unless the arbitral tribunal determines otherwise because of the particular circumstances of the case, the expenses of the tribunal, including the remuneration of its members, shall be borne by the Parties to the dispute in equal shares. The tribunal shall keep a record of all its expenses, and shall furnish a final statement thereof to the Parties.

15. Any Party to this Convention having an interest of a legal nature in the subject-matter of the dispute, and which may be affected by a decision in the case, may intervene in the proceedings with the consent of the tribunal.

16. The arbitral tribunal shall render its award within five months of the date on which it is established unless it finds it necessary to extend the time limit for a period which should not exceed five months.

17. The award of the arbitral tribunal shall be accompanied by a statement of reasons. It shall be final and binding upon all Parties to the dispute. The award will be transmitted by the arbitral tribunal to the Parties to the dispute and to the secretariat. The secretariat will forward the information received to all Parties to this Convention.

18. Any dispute which may arise between the Parties concerning the interpretation or execution of the award may be submitted by either Party to the arbitral tribunal which made the award or, if the latter cannot be seized thereof, to another tribunal constituted for the purpose in the same manner as the first.

TABLE OF CASES

Alfons Lutticke GmbH et al v Commission [1966] Case 48/65, ECR 19......*138*

An Taisce and World Wide Fund for Nature v Commission (1992) Case 407/92, OJ C27, 30.1.93.......*185*

Becker v Finanzamt Munster-Innenstadt [1982] ECR 53.......*114, 123, 138*

Lord Bethell v Commission [1982], Case 246/81, ECR 2277........*127*

Bund Naturschutz and others v Bavarian Higher Regional Court, ECJ Case C-396/92......*141*

Canadian Wildlife Federation v Canada (1989) 3 F.C. 309, 3 CELR (NS.) 287, affirmed (1989) 4 CELR (NS.) 1)........*46*

von Colson and Kamman v Land Nordrhein Westfalen [1984] ECR 1891.......*121*

Costanzo v Commune di Milano (1989) Case 103/88, Judgement of ECJ 22 June 1989...........*118*

EC Commission v Belgium [1982] CMLR 627.......*74*

Emmot v Minister for Social Welfare (1991) Case 208/90, Judgement of ECJ 25 July 1991.........*124*

Laurel Heights Improvement Association of San Francisco, Inc. v The Regents of the University of California, C.A. Ist, Nos. A052852 & A052853, May 12 1992.............*87*

Lewin and Rowley v Secretary of State for the Environment and Secretary of State for Transport (1989), 2 JEL 216 (1990).........*113*

Marleasing v La Commercial Internacional de Alimentacion [1990] ECR 4135.....*120, 121*

Michael Brown v An Bord Pleanala (High Court of Eire, 27 July 1989), 2 JEL 209 (1990).....*117*

Petition of Kincardine and Deeside District Council (Court of Session, 8 March 1991) 4 JEL 289 (1992).......*73, 115, 123*

R v Poole Borough Council ex parte Bee Bee and others (1990) 3 JEL 293 (1991)......*119, 122*

R v Secretary of State for the Environment ex parte Rose Theatre Trust (1989) 2 WLR 186 [1990]; 2 JEL 231 (1990)........*125*

R v Secretary of State for Transport ex parte Factortame Ltd [1991] 1 All ER 70......*124*

R v Secretary of State for Transport ex parte Surrey County Council (1993), High Court, 24 November 1993, unreported.....*122, 142*

R v Swale Borough Council and the Medway Ports Authority ex parte RSPB (1990) 3 JEL 135 (1991)..........*120, 123*

Sierra Club v Morton (1972) 405 U.S. 727.........*97*

Twyford Parish Council v Secretary of State for the Environment and Secretary of State for Transport (1990) 4 JEL 274 (1992)........*111, 123*

TABLE OF EU LEGISLATION

Council Directive on the assessment of the effects of certain public and private projects on the environment 85/337/EEC.......*15-20, 24-33, 34-40, 48-78, 79-83, 93-5, 105-6, 110-127, 131-142, 144-6, 183, 186, 187-8*

Council Directive on the conservation of wild birds 79/409/EEC (the Birds Directive)........*58*

Council Directive on the conservation of natural habitats and of wild fauna and flora 92/43/EEC.........*58*

Council Directive on freedom of access to environmental information 90/313/EEC........*86-7*

Council Directive 84/360/EEC - the Air Framework Directive..........*199*

Council Directive 88/609/EEC - Large Combustion Plants Directive.......*200*

Council Regulations EEC No. 2081/93 and 2082/93 (Structural Fund framework and co-ordination regulations).........*185*

Proposal for a Council Directive on integrated pollution prevention and control COM (93) 423 final, 14 September 1993.........*199*

Treaty of Rome 1957 (and as amended).........*15-16, 18, 83, 118*

TABLE OF STATUTES

Australia Environmental Protection (Impact of Proposals) Act 1974.......*15*

California Environmental Quality Act (CEQA) 1970.......*44-5, 87-8, 98, 143, 148-150*

Canadian Environmental Assessment Act (CEAA) 1992....*45-7, 151*

Electricity Act 1989........*69-70, 133-4*

Environmental Protection Act 1990:

Part I........*194-7, 200-203*

European Communities Act 1972:

s.2....*48-9, 52-3, 77*

Forestry Act 1967.......*73*

Harbours Act 1964.......*78*

Highways Act 1980.......*62, 114*

Malaysia Environmental Quality Act 1974.......*189*

National Parks and Access to the Countryside Act 1949......*64*

Netherlands Environmental Protection (General Provisions) Act 1986......*94*

New Roads and Street Works Act 1991.......*63*

New Zealand Resource Management Act 1991.......*100, 143, 151-2*

Planning and Compensation Act.......*174*

s.10......*59*
s.15......*30, 49, 52, 63, 72, 77*

Planning (Listed Buildings and Conservation Areas) Act 1990........*63*

Supreme Court Act 1981........*124*

Town and Country Planning Act 1990:

s.71A........*52*

Transport and Works Act 1992.........*78*

US Clean Air Act 1963......*97*

US National Environmental Policy Act (NEPA) 1969........*15, 20, 25-7, 40-45, 96-100, 103, 143, 148, 150*

Water Resources Act 1991.........*197*

Wildlife and Countryside Act 1981......*63*

TABLE OF STATUTORY INSTRUMENTS

Canadian Enviromental Assessment and Review Process Guidelines Order 1984............*46, 100, 150-151*

Electricity (Application for Consent) Regulations 1990 (SI No. 455).......*82*

Electricity and Pipe-line Works (Assessment of Environmental Effects) Regulations 1990 (SI No. 442)............*50, 69-71, 132*

Environmental Assessment (Afforestation) Regulations 1988 (SI No. 1207).............*50, 72-5, 115*

Environmental Assessment (Salmon Farming in Marine Waters) Regulations 1988 (SI No. 1218)............*50, 77*

Environmental Assessment (Scotland) Regulations 1988 (SI No. 1221).......*50*

Environmental Information Regulations 1992 (SI No. 3240)..........*87*

Environmental Protection (Prescribed Processes and Substances) Regulations 1991 (SI No. 472) and as amended by SI 1991 No. 836, SI 1992 No. 614, SI 1993 No. 1749 and SI 1993 No. 2405.............*196*

Environmental Protection (Applications, Appeals and Registers) Regulations 1991 (SI No. 507).............*196*

Environmental Protection (Authorisation of Processes) (Determination Periods) Order (No. 513) 1991..............*196*

Harbour Works (Assessment of Environmental Effects) Regulations 1988 (SI No. 1336)..............*50, 78*

Harbour Works (Assessment of Environmental Effects) (No. 2) Regulations 1989 (SI No. 424)..............*50*

Highways (Assessment of Environmental Effects) Regulations 1988 (SI No. 1241)..............*50, 62-8, 111-14*

Land Drainage Improvement Works (Assessment of Environmental Effects) Regulations 1988 (SI No. 1217)..............*50, 76*

NEPA Code of Federal Regulations (CFR) title 40, s.1501-8...........*41, 97*

Town and Country Planning (Assessment of Environmental Effects) Regulations 1988 (SI No. 1199)...........*31, 49, 51-58, 62, 68-71, 80-82, 93, 119-121, 198-9*

Town and Country Planning (Assessment of Environmental Effects) (Amendment) Regulations 1990 (SI No. 367)..........*49, 70-71*

Town and Country Planning (Development Plan) Regulations 1991 (SI No. 2794)..............*174*

Town and Country Planning General Development Order 1988 (SI No. 1813)..............*50, 57-61, 62*

Town and Country Planning (General Development) (Scotland) Amendment Order 1988 (SI No. 977)...........*50*

Town and Country Planning (General Development) (Scotland) Amendment No. 2 Order 1988 (SI No. 1249)............*50*

Transport and Works (Applications and Objections Procedure) Rules 1992 (SI No. 2902)..............*78*

INDEX

Agenda 21..........*178-80, 205*

Alternatives..........*24-5, 43-4, 54-5, 67, 96, 157-8, 198-9, 204*

An Taisce..........*184*

Best Available Techniques Not Entailing Excessive Cost (BATNEEC)......*195, 199-200, 202-3*

Best Practicable Environmental Option (BPEO).........*24, 195, 203*

British Herpetological Society (BHS)........*119, 122*

Burren Action Group.........*184-5*

California State Clearinghouse........*45, 98*

Canford Heath.........*119-20, 122*

Channel Tunnel Rail Link........*126-7, 136*

China...........*90-91, 204*

Cost Benefit Analysis (COBA)......*66-7*

Council for the Protection of Rural England (CPRE)..........*49, 93, 137, 146, 196*

Cumulative impacts.........*108, 150*

Department of Transport Departmental Standard HD 18/88.......*63-68, 139*

Designated areas............*31, 61, 63-4, 109-10*

EIA Directive

direct effect...........*32, 52, 114-18*
five-year review............*36-40, 105-7*

legal basis......*18, 27*
requirements of...........*35-40*

Enforcement ('ombudsman') agency.......*93, 98-102*

Environmental appraisal..........*64*

Environmental assessment..........*11, 43, 112*

Environmental impact assessment (EIA)..........see also SEA

best practice.........*23-4*
birth of........*14*
definition..........*22-4*
terminology..........*11*

Environmental impact report (EIR).........*44-5, 87-88, 150*

Environmental (impact) statement (EIS/ES)........*20, 35, 41-4, 53, 63, 66-69, 80-85, 92, 93-8, 103, 104, 132-4, 168-9, 194*

Environmental Impact Tables (EITs)........*65-6*

Environmentalism.........*13*

European Community

environmental policy..........*15, 83*
Environment Action Programmes.............*16-18*
Fifth Action Programme.........*181-3*
infringement action..........*75, 82, 126*
Structural Funds..........*184-6*

FEARO........*46-7, 100*

Flue Gas Desulphurisation (FGD)..........*200-203*

Forestry Commission.......*72-5, 115-6*

Glendye..............*115-7, 123*

Her Majesty's Inspectorate of Pollution (HMIP)........*193-7, 203*

India..........*91, 190*

Kenya........*189*

Litigation........*20, 94, 97-9, 109-127*

Malaysia........*189*

Manual of Environmental Appraisal (MEA)..........*64-8, 139-141*

Mitigation...........*22, 45, 54, 66-7, 104-6*

National Rivers Authority (NRA)........*30, 74, 76, 169*

Nature Conservancy Council (English Nature).......*119*

Netherlands EIA Commission......*38, 94, 99*

Objectives-led policy formulation.....*153-176*

Overseas Development Administration (ODA)......*190*

Oxleas Wood..........*126, 138*

Parliamentary bills...........*48*

Permitted development rights........*58-61, 71*

Planning Policy Guidance note 12 (PPG 12)........*174-6*

Policy appraisal........*146-7, 163, 166, 170-76*

Primary legislation............*49, 52*

Programmatic EIS/EIR.............*148-150*

Rio Earth Summit........*11, 12, 163, 178, 191, 207*

Royal Society for the Protection of Birds (RSPB).........*120, 123-4*

Scoping...........*84-5, 92, 94, 146*

Strategic environmental assessment (SEA)

definition........*11, 22-4, 130, 170*
draft EC Directive..........*11, 144-146*
role in sustainable development..........*10-12, 145, 153-176, 179-80, 191-2, 204-7*

Thresholds and criteria..........*28-33, 38, 49, 60-61*

Trans-European Road Network (TERN)........*186*

Twyford Down.........*111-14, 123, 126-7, 138*

UK Sustainability Strategy........*11, 164, 180-1*

UN Environment Programme (UNEP).....*14*

US Council on Environmental Quality (CEQ)............*41, 96-9*

Wednesbury unreasonableness.........*115, 121*

World Bank...........*90-91, 190-1*

World Wide Fund for Nature (WWF).........*119, 122, 184, 197*

ADDENDUM

New Legislation

On 18 March 1994 the UK Government finally announced that the long-awaited regulations to extend the application of EIA to projects not covered by the EC Directive (pp 30, 49, 63, 77) would come into force on 8 April 1994. However, in an extraordinary volte-face, which appears to reflect the deregulation initiative rather than any commitment to sustainability, the regulations will apply only to wind turbines, coastal protection works, motorway service areas and toll roads. They will not apply, as the Government had originally proposed, to trout farms, golf courses, non-motorway service areas or drinking water treatment plants - many of the developments which persuaded the Government to legislate in the first place. Ironically, in the same week the European Commission approved its much-delayed proposals for strengthening the EIA Directive.

Direct effect of EIA Directive

Wychavon District Council v Secretary of State for the Environment and Velcourt Ltd (Times Law Report, 7.1.94, ENDS 228).

A planning application by Velcourt Ltd for poultry houses and dwellings for agricultural workers in Hereford had been refused by the local authority, but granted on appeal by a planning inspector. The application had been made on 11 July 1988: after the 3 July deadline when the Directive should have come into force, but before the Town and Country Planning (Assessment of Environmental Effects) Regulations 1988 came into force on 15 July. Mr Justice Tucker rightly rejected the argument that the directly effective nature of the EIA Directive should apply to the private developers: that would give the Directive horizontal effect. Why the district council did not attempt to apply the direct effect doctrine against the Secretary of State or the planning inspector as emanations of the state is not clear. Mr Justice Tucker also considered whether the provisions of the

Directive were, in any case, sufficiently precise and unconditional to have direct effect. He held that if any Article lacked precision - and he identified a number - then the Directive as a whole was incapable of having direct effect. This view contradicts that of the European Commission and previous cases (p114). The fact that the project in question was an Annex II project (see p116) was not addressed. The applicants also attempted to invoke the doctrine of sympathetic interpretation (p121), but the Court declined to apply it.

Habitats Directive

Article 6 (3) of the Habitats Directive (92/43/EEC), due to come into force in June 1994, requires an "appropriate assessment" of the implications of plans or projects likely to have significant effects on a site covered by the Directive, "in view of the site's conservation objectives". While a step in the right direction, it represents one element only of what a full SEA would cover. The UK Government, in its consultations on implementing the Habitats Directive, has so far chosen to ignore the reference to plans in Article 6 (3).

William Sheate

22 March 1994